CENTRE FOR EDUCATIONAL RESEARCH AND INNOVATION

MAKING
THE CURRICULUM WORK

ORGANISATION FOR ECONOMIC CO-OPERATION AND DEVELOPMENT

ORGANISATION FOR ECONOMIC CO-OPERATION AND DEVELOPMENT

Pursuant to Article 1 of the Convention signed in Paris on 14th December 1960, and which came into force on 30th September 1961, the Organisation for Economic Co-operation and Development (OECD) shall promote policies designed:

- to achieve the highest sustainable economic growth and employment and a rising standard of living in Member countries, while maintaining financial stability, and thus to contribute to the development of the world economy;
- to contribute to sound economic expansion in Member as well as non-member countries in the process of economic development; and
- to contribute to the expansion of world trade on a multilateral, non-discriminatory basis in accordance with international obligations.

The original Member countries of the OECD are Austria, Belgium, Canada, Denmark, France, Germany, Greece, Iceland, Ireland, Italy, Luxembourg, the Netherlands, Norway, Portugal, Spain, Sweden, Switzerland, Turkey, the United Kingdom and the United States. The following countries became Members subsequently through accession at the dates indicated hereafter: Japan (28th April 1964), Finland (28th January 1969), Australia (7th June 1971), New Zealand (29th May 1973), Mexico (18th May 1994), the Czech Republic (21st December 1995), Hungary (7th May 1996), Poland (22nd November 1996) and Korea (12th December 1996). The Commission of the European Communities takes part in the work of the OECD (Article 13 of the OECD Convention).

The Centre for Educational Research and Innovation was created in June 1968 by the Council of the Organisation for Economic Co-operation and Development and all Member countries of the OECD are participants.

The main objectives of the Centre are as follows:

- *analyse and develop research, innovation and key indicators in current and emerging education and learning issues, and their links to other sectors of policy;*
- *explore forward-looking coherent approaches to education and learning in the context of national and international cultural, social and economic change; and*
- *facilitate practical co-operation among Member countries and, where relevant, with non-member countries, in order to seek solutions and exchange views of educational problems of common interest.*

The Centre functions within the Organisation for Economic Co-operation and Development in accordance with the decisions of the Council of the Organisation, under the authority of the Secretary-General. It is supervised by a Governing Board composed of one national expert in its field of competence from each of the countries participating in its programme of work.

Publié en français sous le titre :

PROGRAMMES SCOLAIRES : MODE D'EMPLOI

FOREWORD

Since its creation, CERI (Centre for Educational Research and Innovation) has given continuing priority to the study of the curriculum in all its aspects. Besides an unbroken series of framework activities on fundamental and topical concerns, it has conducted a wide variety of other activities that have illustrated particular facets, such as the pedagogical and organisational implications of applying new information technology to classroom practice, or introducing environmental education into the range of studies. In the 1970s and 1980s, there was a detailed analysis of the early years of pre-schooling, considerations of the transition of young people into working life, the publication of Piagetian inventories, and above all the attention to the organisation of what was for many the start of a new life in secondary schooling. If there was any lack of detailed analysis, it had to do with poor consideration of primary schooling.

An important milestone in CERI consideration of curriculum as such was reached with the report produced in 1990, *Curriculum Reform: An Overview of Trends* (OECD/CERI, 1990), in response to case studies and reports submitted by Member countries. Arising from the report, a major conference on the "Curriculum Redefined" was held at the OECD headquarters in 1993 and participants were asked to consider its findings in five areas: Learning to Think, Thinking to Learn; Core Curriculum; Student Assessment and Evaluation; Science, Mathematics and Technology Education; Humanities, Arts and Values. In 1994, the OECD published a report on the findings, *The Curriculum Redefined: Schooling for the 21st Century* (OECD/CERI, 1994).

These studies have provided the context and the *modus operandi* of the recent CERI project on "Teachers and Curriculum Reform in Basic Schooling", initiated in 1994, which led to the preparation of this report. Two broad assumptions underpinned the approach taken. First, it was agreed that the conclusions would be addressed to policy-makers and to others who can influence directions of change, recognising that many factors affect the way in which policy changes are implemented. Second, the discussions and ideas were developed in recognition that there are no unique answers to the questions that might be posed; the significance of an issue, and the value of possible ways of responding to it, are often closely dependent on the particular national and cultural context. The project focused on the three complementary cluster issues of *curriculum reform, assessment and accountability,* and the *professional development of teachers.* Its purpose was to collect and synthesize a rich mass of information from the countries under review, and from other studies on the state of the art, to suggest key issues and developments and give pointers for possible future work. In addition, further reflection on equity and action on low achievement was sought across these three cluster areas.

Each of these areas was considered by a separate group (see Annex for group membership). The three groups drew up their own framework of issues, illustrated by examples in different countries drawn from the experiences of the participating members of the groups. Moreover, the analysis in this volume drew on other OECD education work, as is reflected in the overview; for example, on Indicators, School Failure, The Teacher Today, Human Resources and Country Reviews. In 1995, the OECD published *Performance Standards in Education: In Search of Quality* (see OECD, 1995a), a report on how ten Member countries define, modernise, monitor and evaluate standards of performance in school. Recent reviews of national policies for education have proved a fruitful source of evidence on major trends and issues. Particular account is taken of the need to respond to the wish of the OECD Ministers of Education, expressed at their last quinquennial meeting in January 1996, that all education policies and practices should be designed to facilitate the creation of lifelong learning societies. Thus basic schooling is seen, not as an end in itself, but as the platform on which to build continuing lifelong learning. The current CERI programme reflects this emphasis within the activity Schooling for Tomorrow, which is examining the foundational role of school in supporting the concept of lifelong learning, with attention to the context of schools as they enter the 21st century, good practice and innovation, methodologies for addressing change and alternative future scenarios, and the particular impact of information and communication technology. The groups reported with a diversity of style and detail of coverage, and these original reports have been edited into the chapters of this volume. They are introduced by a Secretariat overview. It draws significantly upon the reports of the three studies, as well as the unpublished documentation collected during the life of the activity, including additional work on systemic reform and the records of their meetings. The overview seeks to put these broad themes in context and to draw out some main strands and conclusions; it emphasizes the comparative nature of the study by pointing up contrasts and common features, while relating these to theories, models and typologies wherever feasible.

The Secretariat is indebted to those who co-ordinated and contributed to the work under the three clusters (see Annex), and, in preparing the overview and editing, to John Lowe (formerly of the OECD Secretariat) and Maurice Holt (University of Colorado, Denver, United States), acting as consultants. Over and above the input of time and commitment of the many individuals involved, the work enjoyed the generous financial support of the US Department of Education.

The report is published on the responsibility of the Secretary-General of the OECD.

TABLE OF CONTENTS

AN OVERVIEW OF KEY ISSUES ARISING

CURRICULAR AIMS, PRINCIPLES AND STRUCTURES

The context

Quality or excellence has continued to be a dominant theme in educational discourse, with a renewed emphasis on standards of student performance and the effectiveness of teaching. The problems of achieving more equal access to education and fairer chances for all to benefit from its outcomes have also come to exercise teachers, policy-makers and the research community, causing the concept of relevance to real life to emerge as a major consideration. Thus, the search is on for educators to find ways of engaging the interests and energies of every student, to reduce school failure and drop-out rates, and to raise the standards of all engaged in schooling.

OECD education systems have to cope with basic changes to their environment if new expectations are themselves to be created from the different stakeholders either within or outside the formal system. Societies are tending to erode central control and hand over responsibilities to the schools. Every student is now expected to reveal more activity, more responsibility and a greater learning drive than in the past. Some key challenges arise:

- a rapidly evolving world, particularly because of the acceleration of technological progress in the field of communication, has two direct implications for education: the needs, first to clarify the common core of knowledge and skills that all young people require before embarking on adult life, and second to prepare the minds of the young for constant adaptation to new conditions in their lives as adults;

- education for all implies special efforts to help the under-served so that they may realise their full potential, whereby all the pools of talent in a country are tapped;

- a globalisation of the economy with greater interaction between countries, and a premium on human adaptability and flexibility, suggests the necessity of acquiring novel types of skills and competences and being able to deal with multiculturalism;

- the development of management paradigms within organisations requires a mobilisation of fresh competences at all levels and an increase of the general level of educational attainment of the whole labour force.

These four challenges all suggest the importance of implementing education as a lifelong learning process. Alongside these are at least the following outstanding problem areas:

- a durable slowdown of economic growth in certain industrialised countries, with some minorities cumulating social handicaps, especially in urban areas; in these areas it is expected that the school should contribute significantly to overcoming disadvantage;

- a predominance of materialistic values which leads certain young people to lose sight of existential landmarks, to fall into serious problems like drug addiction, or to reach out for certain extremist reactions – sects, fundamentalism, racism – all of which threaten peace on both the domestic and international scenes. There is a moral dimension here;

- a threat to the ecological balance of our planet which calls for more awareness of the environmental issues and more concern for sustainable economic growth.

A curriculum for all

A useful starting point for re-evaluating the curriculum is the quest for opportunities for all, with the further implication of differentiation according to the abilities of each student. A curriculum is meant here to cover the entire body of courses, including play, dramatic presentations and other recreational offerings, provided by a given school. Radical responses to the need for curriculum growth are inhibited by the limits of location, space and time that are traditionally built into the school. Still, learning outcomes are everywhere receiving special emphasis, as countries seek to redefine the aims and goals of schooling. They are including inter-disciplinary problem-solving, creative initiative, flexibility and adaptability to address change, ability to work in groups, and an intelligent interest in technology – its uses, limitations and demands on social responsibility. A background consideration for this activity was the declaration of the OECD Ministers of Education at their meeting in 1990 of a need for coherence and focus to avoid curriculum overload. The widening range of tasks and clienteles calls for a rich variety of offerings and of teaching methods, to ensure that all students can experience programmes that meet their talents and interests.

None of this is to deny a considerable element of commonality for all students. Several interconnecting themes continue to arise – between disciplinary and inter-disciplinary approaches, between cognitive and non-cognitive aims, between vocational and academic considerations, and between the responsibility to meet social needs and the duty of serving the development of individuals. The desire of many schools – to contribute to a programme of mass education for all, but at the same time to match the diverse needs of students coming from many different backgrounds – must be rooted in broad guidelines, syllabuses and text materials.

The academic/vocational tension in particular has received extensive attention. Progress here might lie in strengthening the core that is common across different tracks and in providing second chances. Students could thus move from one option to another, thereby improving the quality of their education. By organising fewer tracks, all built around broad groups of skills and all with a focus on the problem-solving needed in people's lives, more core skills can be imagined. If these principles were pursued effectively, the differences between the tracks would be reduced. The main problems would then be those of overload, for example, how to set standards for vocational competence while achieving the optimal level of academic performance for national or regional standards.

How then to create genuinely equal opportunities while recognising the differences that exist among students? How to ensure that students of modest ability maintain their motivation and development? There is a marked difference between, for example, the *German* approach, with its tripartite system, and the many countries with largely common provision up to the end of lower secondary education, and frequently beyond. Countries will probably agree that the following need to be considered:

- the priority goals of schooling and the type of curriculum to be implemented at different ages;

- the best structuring of educational streams and organisation of learning pathways;

- the aims and means for suitable career guidance measures for all students;

- the means for improving the quality of teachers whose task is becoming more and more arduous;

- the means to enhance participation of all students and parents in the learning process;

- the most appropriate uses of educational and information technologies and how to put these in place;

- the best ways to steer and manage education systems, given the need to encourage innovation, grassroots initiatives and overall consistency.

What is the optimum degree of decentralisation and autonomy expected of schools in order to increase their ability to innovate, without increasing geographical and social inequalities? What are the most effective methods for regulating and steering at all levels of decision-making from the classroom to the national level? Any strategy of change must take into account the lessons from the past. The constant shortfalls are well known between policy-makers' intentions and the actual implementation of policy, the gap between rhetoric and reality, the problems of implementing top-down reforms and of making local reform work by extending grassroots initiatives.

The school should continue to transform itself, not only to adapt to the changing environment but to prepare for a more relevant future. For example, many are struggling to resolve the combat between the need of the nation-state for unity and cohesion and the desire for greater autonomy in the plurality of communities of which each state is composed. There is also growing pressure for young people to be given more responsibility in defining their own futures. In framing aims for the schools, education authorities are not always clear about those essential qualities which should be promoted in the citizens of the future.

Many young people are increasingly fed in passive ways by the media. Too many are experiencing only a little of the emotional support and care that stable families or other adult groups can provide. In the worst situations, the weak family and community support goes with low employment prospects and an absence of long-term hope. These features all have the effect of burdening many schools and their teachers with responsibility for dealing with increasingly difficult situations. Thus, societies are looking for more from their schools than in the past. If some want to prescribe and control education out of fear that schools may not have the will or the capacity to respond to the public's needs, others want schools to be less protective and to enjoy more autonomy. There is a tension here that needs to be resolved.

New levels of government and public attention

Educational reform, directed at qualitative improvement in student learning, is as old as the establishment of schools as public institutions. In the period of major growth in provision and expectations in many Member countries' school systems, mainly in the 1950s and 1960s, prominence was given to interventionist strategies on the entire school system. In certain countries, there was a heightened concern over standards. The interventions indicate a tendency to take up a succession of system-wide strategies, based on identification of selected forces or legal instruments capable of being directly enlisted at the school level. Even so, it is only in very recent years that qualitative improvement of students' performance overall has become a major preoccupation of governments. There is, today, a broad consensus within OECD governments upon the main goals of education:

- transmission of essential knowledge and skills and a basis of common culture;
- development of personalities both at the individual level and collectively, so as to contribute to democratic values and citizenship;
- preparation for working life that not only leads to a first job, but to the acquisition of skills for many jobs;
- giving better chances to those with social and individual disabilities.

But there is a problem. Politicians tend naturally to adopt a programmatic and short-term approach to issues and it is hard to see how this trend can be reversed. Education officials may not agree on essentials and tend also to look for quick answers. It is far from easy to reach a consensus upon the relative weight which should be given to each of the above four goals. Some say that there is a need for transparent debate on such a fundamental social issue as what is meant by a good education for all. Whatever the answer to weighing the goals of education, once they have been accepted, it should be clear that education is not only a private invest-ment in human capital but also a matter of deep public concern. Education can have very positive effects for social cohesion and welfare as well as for economic efficiency; it must continue to exercise these effects. An important consequence that follows is that regulation of the education system cannot rely upon a pure mar-ket mechanism but has to be multi-faceted. The social capital that people bring to the school is much less sure than it used to be. However, this is not a problem that schools should, even when theoretically able, try to tackle in isolation from their communities. Such isolation is, however, all too common. Positive initiatives are called for to involve local communities or jurisdictions in order to make schools more responsive to people's needs and to use more fully out-of-school services.

A particular challenge for schools is to strike a balance between their time-honoured role as guardians and transmitters of established culture and their new role of preparing students for what looks like an uncertain future. Notably, there is the conflict between nationalism and the attitudes required for internation-alism to help resolve old conflicts. Paradoxically, a strong confidence in one's own traditions may support the readiness to give up some aspects of one's way of living. A key question is how governments and schools, in the face of unavoidable public spending constraints can bring about change, so as to increase the general level of educational attainment. Both equity and effectiveness are called for. If certain social minorities are to avoid the disproportionate experience of failure, it is essen-tial to increase mass education at secondary and tertiary levels, while maintaining respectable standards of quality. One particular aspect is how to ensure good recruits to high-skill jobs, without giving rise to the sort of discrimination that appears to be incompatible with the goals of equity and social cohesion.

For further consideration

How is the school to be in touch with labour market demands and how is it to decide on the best way to organise the future learning of its students?

If adults will in future be increasingly finding work in *ad hoc* contracts rather than in permanent employment, they will be more mobile and depend increasingly on portfolios, based on their previous various jobs with samples of their work. How should schools reflect this trend and prepare their students for working in this way?

Should the school be teaching and examining students in moral education, in a broad understanding of their duties as citizens, and in their attitudes to their school work and to their lives as a whole?

Analyses might focus on the processes by which standards are established and how these differ among cultures with a wealth of varying inputs. The forces that drive change at different times should also be better understood.

Quality, standards and equity

Education is a complex process which involves many players within a system. Hence, there can be no overarching theory of how educational provision operates, which explains why the common recourse is to use stylistic imagery, and why the common conceptual framework within which an agreement can be reached is the input/output model with the processes still hidden inside the "black box". It is possible and desirable, however, to take into account important interactions between the key components. For instance, the objectives and the structure of the curriculum should be matched to the assessment procedures, and the required attitudes related to the role and abilities of teachers and students. The mere addition of a cross-curricular option cannot be easily made to work without using several collaborating teachers. It is essential to have inter-disciplinary teams of teachers reflecting on real local needs. The model of learning first, and application thereafter, should be replaced by one in which reflection on real life situations may be used as a mode of learning to overcome the disconnection between theory and practice.

Some particular efforts are worth noting. The first is the effort to change the curriculum in response to new knowledge, including awareness of how students can learn effectively and how changes can take place in society. Good examples can come from either top-down or bottom-up approaches and from the initiatives of non-educators. The second concerns cross-curricular developments. Effective implementation and assessment need to be achieved using teams of teachers. The priority should be to develop the habit of lifelong learning rather than to restructure subject areas. If inter-disciplinary themes are considered to be important, then it is necessary to see how to define and realise them, bearing in mind that the term "cross-curricular" may have different meanings from one place to another. Any set of principles should include ideas about linking the theoretical to the practical, and about relating knowledge to values. The school system has to define the common and cross-curricular competences it aims to develop and to show assessment evidence of how they are achieved. The focus on standards is the third preoccupation – how to establish consensus on what standards should be referred to, who should specify them and how they might be realised. Critical issues are the local adaptation and use of national standards, the formulation of criteria applying to both academic and vocational work, and evidence as to whether standards can positively help school improvement. Not only successes but also the lessons to be learned from failures need to be explored.

Getting the right balance in all these efforts between local and national roles in curriculum reform is crucial. In federal countries such as *Australia, Germany, Switzerland* and the *United States*, there are in-built limits to the national role. Nevertheless, all countries experience difficulty in determining how to strike a balance between central responsibility and the need to delegate control to local communities and schools. The use of such terms as "centralisation" or "decentralisation" requires careful definition. What matters is that teachers and their classes should not be unduly constrained. Central authorities can support local responsibilities, for example by promoting teacher networks as in *Belgium* or by sending out teachers to demonstrate new approaches as in *Norway*. If decision-making is to be divided across several levels in the system, the question arises as to how should these activities be co-ordinated.

One way of recognising the levels at which decisions are taken is by considering the documents that support curriculum policy. Many countries publish their general decisions through a statement of *core curriculum*. Some, like those for the Flemish Community in *Belgium* and for *England and Wales*, prescribe content in detail. Some, like that for *Norway*, offer a set of general principles. Others provide a framework with broad pointers, like the set of attainment targets in the *Netherlands*, or the aims and content areas in the new *Finnish* framework and in some *German Länder*. Statements of *guidelines* may be formal, or provide a bridging function between state and school as in *Norway*. Guidelines may also be examples of interpretation, such as the *Dutch* guidelines for the attainment targets. In *Scotland*, statements about the curriculum have been derived from a consultative programme and incorporated in national guidelines for all areas of the curriculum. But the core curriculum is only an indicative frame and what matters is how it is interpreted and applied by schools and teachers.

Effective curriculum reform implies growth from existing practice with schools able to react reflectively on their own progress. A completely novel cross-disciplinary approach may well fail by being too radical, whereas significant reforms can be achieved within traditional subjects, for example through adopting enquiry learning in science. No purely external policy can mandate what can be done. The school is a reconstruction of culture and not just a transmitter of it. The perspective on the curriculum has to make academic sense to all young people, though too often the presentation is not couched in suitable terms.

Equity issues are properly a concern across OECD countries and can be understood as they relate to the three main areas: curriculum change, teacher training, and assessment. Problems of high and long-term unemployment and social exclusion among young people are now evident in many countries, problems that closely correlate with educational attainment. These give additional urgency to equity issues. Countries can respond by addressing initial education through a broad range of actions, reforming curriculum, pedagogy, teacher training and pre-school facilities. Both equity and the national requirements demand that responses be targeted, particularly on young people from disadvantaged families and those with poor results. A student's achievement is conditioned by a combination of the wider social environment, family factors, the school, and his or her own personality. It is important to consider each student's self-image, for if this is low a student is more likely to behave passively or aggressively. For teachers, there is need for awareness of their own possibly prejudiced attitudes towards under-achieving students, and of the importance of adopting strategies to combat learning difficulties as they find them. Models of learning and expectations of pedagogy may be sources of differences between schools and families. The implication is that teachers and schools have to help create shared understanding with parents and carers, for those children who are at risk.

Problems of disability are a particular aspect of "at risk". Some disabilities require expert care, while for several previously thought to be incurable there are new ways to help. Care has to be taken to avoid labelling children as "low ability" or "not gifted". Aims and methods should be set in an inter-cultural perspective. Special advisory teachers should be asked to visit schools to assist with difficult cases. The orientation of the curriculum should also draw upon cultural minorities as a resource rather than risk alienating them. It should work to bring about social coherence and to offer the same prospects of successful achievement to everyone. Motivation of students is a key target. Ethnic minorities have specific problems, particularly in the second and third generation when they hold less strongly to their original culture but are still not fully accepting of those of the adopted country.

Priorities should include better pre-school education and co-operation with the parents so that they can help the teachers.

The issue of cultural heritage, values and national identity remains a potential source of problems and disagreements. To talk of schools serving a common heritage and helping to promote a national identity is offensive in certain countries, where agreement on such issues does not exist and where, in consequence, attempts to impose one on schools would be seen as an attempt by a certain group to marginalise or oppress the cultures of others. Moreover, in many countries the advent of significant ethnic minorities means that the previous common cultural heritage is giving way to a pluralistic society. Schools are arenas in which such cultural conflicts are to be worked out. They cannot be expected to start from ready-made solutions.

Examples of curricular concerns and approaches

The environmental emphasis

CERI work on education and the environment (e.g. OECD/CERI, 1991) has shown how some of the general principles apply in relation to a specific thrust for the curriculum. That study analysed attempts to link the learning of school subjects with experience gained in identifying and analysing problems of living in the local environment. The knowledge and skills acquired in a variety of inter-disciplinary subjects can then be applied in addressing solutions in real contexts. In some instances, students are taken out into the community to discover the attitudes of individuals or the public authorities. The aim is to promote environmental awareness by enabling students themselves to use their initiative and enterprise in identifying issues, designing investigations, collecting and analysing relevant information, developing solutions and reporting their work to the community. The innovative school projects for the CERI study were selected on the basis of certain criteria. They permit activities not only embracing the acquisition of knowledge but also having a discernible influence on the students' human and natural surroundings. Representatives of varying concepts of environmental concerns – social, economic, and cultural – are met, as are the different levels of schools (primary, secondary, and vocational). Activities placed in a variety of geographical locations can take place, and links with institutions outside the school system are organised. It is a difficult task but it does engage the students in the local community.

Insights from OECD national education policy reviews

Recent policy reviews – excluding those in Eastern Europe (see below) – have included Denmark, France, Korea and Mexico. Despite the obvious differences between them, the findings accord with what might be expected almost everywhere. Denmark concentrates on the grade 7-10 students and the necessity of keeping them in education and training until they can find a job. *France* is concerned with the well-known problem of under-achievement and marginalisation of many of the young generation, and the difficulty of finding a place in the labour market for those who leave early. *Korean* reforms have many different facets, but are above all concerned with preparing the young for work. The examiners for *Mexico* identify several major areas of policy concern: equity; relevance; diversity and flexibility; quality assurance; staff renewal and development; financing and steering the system and the institutions. All these reviews show that, while each country is focused on some matters of long-term concern, the future is full of immediate problems having to do with preparing the young for an uncertain future. The challenge is to ensure that many of the young are not left to wonder where they are going, or why they should acquire lifelong learning skills.

Countries in Eastern and Central Europe

In 1992, a three-day conference was organised by the OECD Centre for Co-operation with the Economies in Transition. It concluded that there are urgent short-term economic problems linked to educational deficiencies such as skills shortages, and the need for managers and workers to be creative at the workplace. Since then, a number of education policy reviews have occurred, which show that Eastern and Western countries confront very similar challenges. Such features as the following are common: the classroom must reflect new teaching and learning styles more adapted to active participation by learners at all levels; the pace and content of change can be accelerated if educational reforms are led by social demand; wider use of competence-based learning systems that focus on achieving goals can also increase consumer choice, by making it possible for institutions outside the formal education system to provide education and training.

The *Polish* government has set itself a detailed agenda of educational reform: curricular, pedagogic and evaluative changes; improved participation and retention rates at all levels; expansion and restructuring of higher education and teacher training. The investment in time, effort and resources to achieve such reforms is essential for the long-term well-being of the country. A reformed education system will be the surest base on which the new social order may be built. What makes implementation of reform particularly difficult, however, is the context of economic stringency. Thus, the level of investment in education in general, including the remuneration of teachers, is low – not a situation, of course, unique to *Poland*. In *Russia* current educational aims include: overcoming unduly rigid approaches towards teaching and learning and removing the barriers hindering the course of transition; defining a new and appropriate education system with new textbooks; incorporating a management style that reflects new techniques and technologies; making better provision for initial teacher training and continuing staff development, while creating favourable conditions for its implementation.

Hence, analysis of the national education policy reviews suggests that, while there are many distinctive aspects of history and tradition, there are no great divisions between East and West in aims and problems. Curriculum options, except in the detail, do not offer profound differences in responding to the world outside the school. In terms of policies for producing a well-organised society, countries are looking at very similar phenomena.

For further consideration

What policy initiatives need to be taken to raise the achievements of those now in the bottom 20-30 per cent in our schools?

Do we need to give more flexibility and more room to manoeuvre to every school?

How can tensions among the practical, vocational, personal and academic purposes of education be resolved or minimised?

How should partnerships be developed between schools and others with an interest in, and concern for, the quality of educational provision?

ASSESSMENT AND ACCOUNTABILITY

Assessment

Levels of attainment or competence among children and young people appear to be major reasons for public concern about education. They are the focus of changing government policy in a number of countries. In some countries, policy initiatives are concentrated on formal learning in "core" subjects, specifically mother tongue and mathematics. In others, the new initiatives extend to other curriculum subjects, notably history, foreign or second language and the physical sciences. In others again, policy discussions pay less attention to subject competence or measured attainment levels, which may be quite high comparatively, than to behaviour, attitudes and values, and to the promotion of independent thought and creativity in students. In most countries, concern has been expressed over inhibitions and barriers to learning, and about low-performing students.

The diversity of interests and of policy initiatives that are at stake suggest that there may be different perceptions of quality and standards or at least different policy agendas across OECD Member countries. There is need to clarify what is intended by "quality" and "standards" of student performance. Overall, there may be a mismatch between rhetoric and action: despite manifold pronouncements, there may well actually be more sustained concern over the question of the "best doing still better" than with the percentage of students who fail to reach pre-defined or assumed minimum standards, who drop out of school or perform at a level deemed to be inadequate for their own or society's continuing good. Questions about the quality of student learning experiences and their relevance to changing societal needs underlie the reform endeavours of many education systems across the OECD countries.

While the purposes of assessment and accountability are overlapping, they are not identical, so that each has to be matched to its own set of methods. Such a mix of overlap and distinctiveness inevitably means that the field is a complex one. There is not a necessary conflict, however, between accountability and the needs of learning. It ought to be possible – through partnerships, persistence and professionalism – for all relevant partners, especially teachers, students and parents, to achieve a better understanding of the issues. This in turn could resolve conflicts that are often more about means than ends. For this to work, there would have to be transparency in all aspects of the assessment process.

In some countries, there have been decisive actions to improve assessment in key structures and processes in the schools. For example, there is much greater emphasis than hitherto on stated targets: the attempt to produce hierarchies of competences; age-defined targets of attainment in basic subjects; the achievement of a wider range of test scores, and the promotion of transparency and accountability, including more rigorous observations and evaluation of schools and their ranking in comparative performances. Significant shifts are occurring in relations between government, regional and local bodies and community agencies. New models are emerging of steering systems while sharing responsibilities.

Where countries are moving towards the setting of standards – subject by subject or field by field, with or without the period of monitoring and formal, system-wide testing – these approaches require more concentrated and co-ordinated efforts nationally than has been the rule. They imply a continuity in policy which is a challenge to political environments, where a succession of governments often means quite substantial changes of direction. Even more marked in this regard is the interest in systemic reform: the recognition that large-scale public education systems are highly complex and that a repertoire of strategic objectives is to be articulated, inter-related and maintained consistently over long periods of time if significant effects are to be achieved.

Teachers and their formative role

Since education is a public good and an important tool for social cohesion, there is a need to achieve uniformity of standards in aims and in assessment records. This is not easy to accomplish as customs and practices vary greatly. Even on apparently minor issues, such as bringing teachers to use the same mark scale in the same way, there is a great deal to be done. It may not always help to insist on uniformity because teachers may then use a common scheme in a mechanical way, risking a meaningless formalism. A very positive role can still be accomplished by assessment – in conveying broader aims and intentions, for instance, or in helping to support the professional careers of teachers. Thus a key question is how uniformity can be achieved, and such positive impacts be supported without the risks of stultifying quality. Can national or state policies create space for schools to have some freedom in their assessments?

Formative evaluations are important and under-represented in practice. They tend not to be well recognised in public debate. They are inevitably highly dependent on teachers, who must therefore be able to inspire a degree of public trust if they are to serve the requirements of assessment without raising any doubts about the learning of their students. There are the difficulties that arise because teachers are not usually expert in interpreting the data and anyway may well not have effective strategies to respond to the revealed needs. The criteria for evaluation are also at issue and may well be questioned, especially as these might have to include local social and community needs, and not just those specified nationally. The very term "formative" may be misunderstood. Banks of external, shared assessment exercises could be important in promoting formative methods, especially among teachers who risk replicating their own self-image if outside stimulus is lacking. The emphasis should be on the detailed qualitative outcomes of such assessments. Many teachers need training in the techniques of effective formative and summative work.

Any policy should concentrate on pedagogically valid assessments rather than technical abstractions. Such assessments can be a powerful aid to raising standards of learning, an aid to professional development and to better communications. The limits to teachers' power are set not only by external demands but also internally by the rights of students, who should be able to understand the criteria and procedures used to assess them. Student assessment is crucial for effective learning, but since most teachers' evaluations are made at the end of sections of teaching, it is too late to use them to enhance the quality of learning. Traditionally, assessment has been largely viewed as summative; radical change is needed if a teacher is to make more effective use of formative assessment in responding to the many different needs of the students in a class.

The blanket national tests, introduced in France in 1989 for all children at ages 8, 11 and 16, are worth mentioning here. While these have been summative, with a possible aim of exploring value-added and serving accountability purposes, the first priority has been to make them useful and acceptable to teachers. They have been held at the beginning of the school year with guidance and help in the marking so that teachers could interpret the results in a diagnostic way to guide the next year's teaching. Banks of items have been built up through collaboration between experts and teachers so that the items would be accepted as valid and useful. The results have not been published, but each school had its own results and the national averages for comparison. At a later stage, estimates of "value added" might be attempted at the end of the school year. The overall strategy has been to establish a culture of evaluation among the teaching profession and the public.

Students should feel ownership and take responsibility for their own learning. To do this, however, they must be conscious of what they are being taught and why. Self-directed learning-by-doing should be encouraged. Experience shows that students can learn how to assess themselves, but it may take time and necessitate different teaching styles, with more attention to individual needs. Instead of the teacher giving students inconsistent messages such as "you are responsible" and then "you must do what I tell you to do", they must be given some flexibility to manage their own learning. Self-assessment must provide students both with feedback on subject achievement and with guidance on methods of working. To enhance students' responsibility, teachers might have to make more explicit the nature of the pedagogic contract which might specify both the duties and the rights of students.

Assessments are fraught with possible biases, but are essential to guiding students' development. If they are formative, they may well not be reported to others. Trust between teachers and students is, of course, critical. In assessment, biases may arise in questions and task requirements, through use of inappropriate contexts and language, as has been well researched and documented. Variety is required in the tasks to be achieved, so that in one task or in another, all students might have the opportunity and stimulus to show their capabilities to the full. A graded curriculum could be matched by graded assessments, with the expectation that all learners will be able to exhibit some level of success. Development of formative assessments is essential here to identify at an early stage those who fall behind so as to ensure that they can obtain special help with their difficulties in good time.

Many of these aspects of assessment assume the committed, active involvement of teachers. They assume a degree of trust, recognition of professional status and enough autonomy to give each teacher a fair chance to succeed. These matters vary considerably between countries; the point to emphasise here is that they are not just limited technical issues but closely linked to the status of teachers.

Accountability

The attainment of various criteria of quality can be used to indicate accountability, but a range of questions arises. Are these criteria to be limited to students' examination performance? Should other matters such as better behaviour or reduced truancy also count, since teachers are expected to secure such improvements? Can accountability needs be met within a strategy for curriculum design? How can the results produced also serve as a trigger for school improvement rather than, as too often happens, merely to confirm prejudices? Is it fair to hold schools accountable for performance results if the students have little personal motivation to perform well? Any accountability system gives status to that which it chooses to assess and so influences the system: what are the possibilities to monitor a system – through light sampling, for instance, or inspections – while preserving in-built flexibility?

The public often prefers accountability to be met through some form of external testing, partly because there is trust in traditional methods, partly because new approaches are seen as suspect, and partly because the limitations of external tests are not understood. Certification may be on a scale that is comparable across a whole country and national policy may be expressed through standards and through assessment. Central authorities can use assessments as a means for strategic direction to promote the aims for each individual student. However, a common posture – that attainment can be measured by external tests while leaving schools free to decide how to teach – is to propose a separation that is artificial in practice. External assessment is bound to influence pedagogy. Furthermore, strong external pressure implies that teachers are not to be trusted, and so is detrimental to their status. Yet, external assessment can expose weaknesses that need attention and which might otherwise be ignored. The need to identify special needs early in a student's schooling is particularly important.

Beyond the individual student level, there is also a need for countries to develop strategies for comprehensive programme evaluation. This calls for systematic designs to collect both quantitative data, particularly on students' performances and cost, and qualitative data, on the reactions and opinions of teachers, parents, etc. Part of such a strategy would be to allocate responsibilities for collecting and interpreting data between different levels and agencies. Countries look to other summative assessment results or to broader programme evaluations, to give assurance about the quality of their education systems, about their effectiveness in working to agreed standards and their relevance to national and local needs. At the same time, however, the meanings given to such terms as quality, standards and relevance may themselves be fluid and subject to change.

It is necessary to clarify who wants to know what, to be used for what purpose, if only to avoid the compilation of unnecessary and unwanted information. It needs to be clear what information is needed for effective forms of quality control. Public discussion has addressed the problems, partly technical in nature, about how accountability can accommodate changing national goals. And, redressing the traditional bias towards content at the expense of skills, giving status to "performance" subjects as in the arts and physical education, assessing cross-disciplinary skills, giving information about values and behaviour, are all important considerations.

It is possible to identify priorities for further development. The different levels in play – formative assessment, students' certification and system accountability – should be related together. The different methods for achieving these should be clarified, internally by teachers with external calibration or by external testing. Where school results are publicly announced, what are the effects of such reporting? Do parents make use of such results or not? Is any action taken to help to improve schools with poor performance? More work is needed to support the assessment of the broader aims of education. These are difficult to measure in an objective way and require different approaches according to the models for learning being adopted. Such work might not be readily acceptable in some communities, for example, religious groups might suspect imposition of values. Among aspects of students' work which might be explored are collaboration, effort, self-regulation and self-awareness, tolerance, and self-confidence. For such qualities, it is more evident than ever that they have to be developed in school-family partnerships. They represent a potential area for fostering collaborative work between countries.

For further consideration

If a wide range of aims is to be assessed, by what means, at what expense, and by what shifts in roles, can these be validly reflected in new assessment patterns or in new tests? Is it possible to ensure that assessment information is used as feedback into any revision of the curriculum and how should this be organised?

Teachers' practices, assumptions, concepts and skills in assessment are generally under-developed. How can this be remedied, particularly in respect of formative assessment?

Several issues, notably the polarities between freedom and control, formative and summative roles, external and internal assessment, require clarification. More thought is needed about the type of data that accountability requires, for what is summative for schools is meant to be formative for the education system.

Can the need for broader sets of indicators – to implement comprehensive programme evaluations – be taken more seriously? Can such indicators respond to the desire for assurance about quality, about relevance and about standards for education?

TEACHERS AND THEIR PROFESSIONAL DEVELOPMENT

New challenges for teachers

The responsibility of teachers is more extensive than in the past. They are given a major role in contributing to a whole array of economic, social and cultural issues, which often have their root causes well beyond the school's ambit. Education policies ought to aim to build on the capacity of teachers to bring about change within the school system, using such measures as: strengthening the curricula in initial training courses; special induction courses for beginning teachers; extensive in-service training at all the stages of a teaching career; regular constructive assessments of teacher performance and career incentives. There are extra pressures on the capacity of a school and teachers to adapt to new challenges, but given the opportunity to develop their skills and a framework of external support, teachers can translate their theories into action.

Policies demand more skills, more active co-operation between teachers and other colleagues or interested actors in the community, and more advanced professional attitudes. Targeted programmes such as multiculturalism, gender equality, and the mainstreaming of the disabled represent situations where the role of teachers is dominant. The successful introduction of information technology into classrooms depends on informed and imaginative application by the teacher. But what is the appropriate balance between selection, pre-service education, induction and lifelong professional development, to meet these diverse demands and to promote quality?

Any reform in initial teacher training is not likely to have a significant effect on teaching in schools for some time, and has to work against the tendency of new teachers to adopt the ethos of experienced colleagues. The focus for change has to be on in-service training (INSET), which is expensive. One should study how countries have linked new developments to INSET programmes, who delivers them, how they are evaluated, and whether there is an inspectorate to help the process of training for change. These issues are linked to those of teacher supply. While this might not be perceived as a major problem area in many countries, the teaching force is rapidly ageing and there are continuing problems of recruiting high quality teachers in many places. Some turnover of the teaching force can be helpful, particularly if mature entrants are being encouraged to join, in that it introduces fresh links with the world outside schools. Too low a turnover can be as damaging as a very high one.

It is often repeated that teachers ought to be the leading agents of change, but are instead the main obstacles to it. It is not as simple as this. Those planning change have to acknowledge, in the first place, that teachers are an integral part of educational success. It is unwise to adopt an impatiently rapid approach to reform.   23

Change should be ambitious but measured, in order to involve teachers properly, while resources should be available to them on an adequate scale. Teachers may have to choose between impersonal presentation of systematic knowledge structures and personal involvement in controversy, between the strengths of specialisation and the need to cross disciplinary boundaries, between transmission of knowledge and generation and reflection on it, and between top-down communication and peer organisation. It is not correct to think that those outside school know how to make change effective. The work of teachers in generating new knowledge is more widespread than is generally realised. Support of such change as much as retraining from outside is what is needed. If no incentives are provided, and if teachers are merely treated as deliverers and not as joint owners of the curriculum, they may impede change or may make no effort to implement a proposed reform. They are far more likely to collaborate if they are directly involved in defining the curriculum and its assessment. This implies that space in national guidelines has to be left for teachers to apply their own professional judgement. The Technical and Vocational Education Initiative (TVEI) scheme in the United Kingdom worked well because participation was voluntary and depended on schools putting forward their own plan within the general criteria for the scheme if they wished to be financed.

If teachers are to be empowered to implement reforms, it is necessary to create a supportive climate in their school. The division of powers and responsibilities between external agencies and schools is not easily balanced. Some national developments in information technology have been disappointing because new schemes, although well resourced, have been too detailed, leaving schools with no scope to impress their own creative seal on innovations. However, school autonomy cannot be absolute. Outside support is needed, for example in overcoming the opposition to reform of parents who want schools to remain as they knew them when young. Teachers also require support from networks which enrich practice, help overcome isolation and avoid the stress that goes with innovation. In some countries, teacher unions or professional associations can help fill this role. There are also examples of such bodies taking up in-service training and executive or advisory roles within curriculum and assessment activities.

However, change must focus both on the individual teacher and the school, with control management, teams of teachers, and individuals sharing responsibilities. If an evolutionary model for curriculum change is to be adopted, it implies that teachers participate in a dynamic interaction to it. Teachers should respond through their national, practical experiences and through feedback reports on their interpretations and successes. To carry out its task, a school also needs to take initiatives in its local community and to involve parents, employers and others in its work. A tradition of change has to be established which sees innovation as part of a continuum and not as episodic events. A shift from an abstract and decontextualised to a more direct approach has helped to link work to the students' daily lives. It implies less emphasis on the traditional disciplines and more on the need to respond to the motivations and needs of all students rather than of an elite. Schools are responding in a variety of ways. Some aim to link the disciplines by creating formal links. Some are using contextualised realistic problems as starting points for cross-disciplinary study. Practical reasoning, which is to do with defending a line of action, deserves more attention.

Professional and career development

Informal local groups bringing teachers together regularly over an extended period is one common method of professional development. This can only work if teachers have responsibility and control in working out their own approaches with their peers. However, complete freedom does not work either. Thus, the question of finding effective ways to improve teachers' practice is linked to the question of how to set and implement standards for teachers' professional practice. Policies to support the best methods have to be fashioned. They might well include changes in collective union agreements to ensure support in relation to new structures for promoting desirable trends. The quality assurance that society needs is seen too often at present as a matter of defining standards and then explaining or testing them. An alternative should be the development of accreditation of teachers who are then trusted to carry out their responsibilities.

Is school-based training a key to improvement? Experiments of giving schools more responsibility for initial training are now highlighted. INSET is also increasingly school-based. The concept of a teacher's career development within a given school is important. As against the dominance of the separate university disciplines, creative school-based work is leading to change. The role of research also needs reconsideration. If teachers could act as researchers, then appreciation and use of findings might be more common. The linking of schools into electronic networks can open up peer work between schools. In all of this, two aspects of development, personal and institutional, should be considered. Raising standards of teachers' work could be helped by providing routes to more professional qualifications. Higher degree courses could have a role if they conscientiously applied theory to practice. In some countries, professional bodies are developing other forms of qualification. The overall purpose is sometimes expressed as the formation of the "master teacher". There is a danger here, of course, of setting an unrealistic standard, though targets and rewards leading to a wider career structure are highly desirable.

Any plans for initial training must include ways of helping trainee teachers to restructure the knowledge they have already acquired, since many of them leave tertiary education with views on the transmission of knowledge which do not follow the present understanding of the way students learn. For most purposes, the requirements of initial and in-service training coincide. It follows that training methods designed to serve the process of adaptation must be adjusted to the behaviour and attitudes of experienced teachers. Teachers must possess mastery of the subject matter and be able to transmit it successfully. However, such is the range of demands on subject knowledge that initial training cannot be expected to shoulder the task, which makes INSET a clear priority. But, if continuing professional development is to meet the demand for innovative teaching, it has to help teachers develop such requisite qualities as an ability to collaborate. Methods designed to promote effective group innovation are different from those required to promote individual innovation, but both are equally important. It is necessary to define the competences required in order to put into practice such classroom reforms as the enhancement of cross-disciplinary skills and projects and to test whether they can be achieved. In-service training needs should be defined for each school. Broader issues of career development must also be considered, notably updating every teacher's subject knowledge and the potential of distance learning methods.

There are thus varied needs if teaching and learning are to be pursued in a more professional context, for which the teacher will require time outside the classroom. This suggests an agenda of educational reform. Networks must be developed, whereby teachers in clusters of local schools can meet to discuss matters of common concern. Peer mentoring may occur, and the different interest groups can relate – teachers, inspectors, academics, researchers, employers, and parents. With such interaction and adequate resourcing, teacher involvement in curriculum development will be promoted and the status of teachers respected. It will, for instance, allow the links between curriculum and assessment to be rethought in ways that emphasise their reciprocal interactions, with special attention to developing practical reasoning and qualities relevant to vocationally-oriented education. Moreover, there will be the forum to address the optimum provision for initial teacher training and what is best a matter for INSET, both in respect of a common core of pedagogical issues and specialised subject training for different phases and subjects.

Alongside the promotion of professional development is the need for attention to appraisals, evaluations, and rewards for excellence. The quality of the system must be assured, with reappraisal of the possible contributions to this arising from indicators such as test results and inspection reports, and the specification of other measures of input, process and output. Quality assurance will be a direct consequence of the transparency arising from the networking of concerned parties including the public.

For further consideration

What are the implications, for the professional roles of teachers and their career development, of the adoption of a flexible model of curriculum change?

What changes in resources and expectations, and what new administrative procedures, are needed to make such a flexible model work?

What relationships or networks have to be formed to ensure that feedback is worked within a school, and that a suitable distillation of results is transmitted to all those concerned?

All the questions discussed here have implications for the role of each school in looking after the development of its staff and in transforming itself into a learning society: how should new models for schools be formulated and how are schools to be supported in their efforts to adopt such models for the professional development of their staff?

POLICY CONSIDERATIONS

Most industrialised countries have been seeking to improve the quality of their systems over the past twenty years or more, often with only partial success. Sometimes, the reform endeavour is limited by a failure to see that a change in, say, assessment practices might also call for changes in curriculum and in teaching practice in order to be successful. There is often a gap between what is proposed and what is done. Sometimes, there is a breakdown, including a failure to involve teachers early enough in the reform process, so they feel no sense of ownership and are unwilling to alter their classroom practice or adapt to modifications in school organisation. A mandate for new standards without providing the necessary resources may well be futile.

Furthermore, most of the parties involved should be looking for the same objectives if they are to be successfully implemented. Teachers tend to talk about their intentions for their students, student motivation, the energy with which they approach their tasks, what students are learning and their own job satisfaction. They are unlikely to be concerned why a politician thinks they should change their methods. This is to illustrate the need for effective communication networks between teachers and politicians and, indeed, all those who have any say in the nature of educational provision. Reform strategies are often targeted on, or originate from one set of stakeholders, with a failure to recognise the legitimate concerns of others. Such strategies have left few enduring effects, and procedures for their evaluation have also proved largely ineffective. Feedback about how the reforms are being implemented is very often cumbersome, and does not help to determine the shape that they should take in the long term. All these limitations and interactions suggest the need to explore more systemic approaches to reform.

The systemic approach

Thus, the education system is complex, variegated, inter-connected and not easily disposed to assume a new appearance. In the light of this, the notion of *systemic reform* has been inspired by the well-known observation that changes affecting any element of the education service can have an effect on some or all other elements, often in a quite unexpected fashion. Significant change in one respect might often require action on all these elements.

The political contexts and motivation for transformation vary considerably. Nevertheless, many countries are moving towards a more systemic approach to reform, which sets goals or standards for good levels of performance in all schools and seeks to provide a coherent set of policies for the improvement of teaching and learning. The idea has its origins in the search for continuous improvement, teacher professionalism, and less hierarchical organisational structures. It assumes a high degree of flexibility and interaction within institutions and a focus on outcomes. These features reflect contemporary thinking about effective management, particularly in business.

In line with the wide variations in political contexts and motivation, there are diverse approaches to implementing more systemic reform. The approaches are in some cases teacher-initiated, while in others they are standards-driven or curriculum-driven. *Teacher-initiated* reform gives priority to the professional development of teachers in the belief that successful innovation depends above all on the motivation and creativity of teachers and schools. Teacher networks are often seen today as one of the major vehicles, not only for sustaining reform but initiating it. *Standards-driven* reform emphasises outcomes in the form of performance standards and gives strategic priority to quality control. *Curriculum-driven* reform tends to focus on pedagogy and subject content and on the relevance of education to the world of work and adult life. The process of curriculum reform is continuous, as content and presentation are adjusted in response to the emergence of new economic signals from the job market or to the needs of hitherto excluded groups of students. At the same time, the influence of developments in higher education on school curricula can exert contradictory pressures. In some countries, concern for standards at school-leaving level has led to a renewed focus on basic subjects and a core curriculum, sometimes at the expense of innovations designed to adapt the curriculum to match changing socio-economic needs.

Substantial evidence shows that many students are capable of learning better and significantly more than they do now. Learning is improved when they are really actively involved and when they take responsibility for what they do. The reconstruction of programmes so that students are challenged by tasks that are realistic leads to more productive modes of learning; so, too, does an increased emphasis on such aspects as co-operation, team work and the practical knowledge that are required in modern workplaces and in everyday life. These factors bring teaching and learning into focus as areas demanding reform and renewal. All this requires a more varied pedagogy. The teachers' vision of learning and modes of relating to their students have to adapt; and such adaptation can make them feel threatened. At the same time, there is a growing recognition that if the role of teachers is enhanced, then the social cohesion within a school and its link with the local community may also be enhanced.

These factors lead to tensions between the simple image of the school as a production line, with sharp divisions of functions and high degrees of specialisation, and economic and social demands for a more inclusive school that emphasises practical reasoning and community studies. How could the design of schools be modified to minimise these tensions? Are there other design approaches that would increase the quality of learning? What is the school's role in deciding how to amend the curriculum?

As seen, curriculum reforms cannot be carried through effectively without the understanding and commitment of teachers. Yet, in the absence of prior consultation and appropriate incentives, teachers are likely to resist most change from whatever pressure group and not to implement curriculum reforms proposed by education authorities at whatever level. It is important, therefore, that they be given some sense of power over innovation. They must feel, in addition, that they are not labouring in isolation but in a fully supportive environment. Policies for curriculum reform should include, therefore, measures to reinforce the capacity of schools to help their teachers become more effective. Curriculum reform also demands the careful alignment of assessment systems, an area in which many teachers are not sufficiently skilled.

Recognising that traditional methods are inadequate to reflect and reinforce the efforts of schools to achieve new aims, several countries are exploring different ways of combining external evaluation measures with measures fashioned by teachers from classroom evidence, such as portfolios of students' work. These efforts encounter difficult problems as they attempt to reconcile the new requirements of validity with the stringency of reliability and comparability across schools. However, schools stand to gain by sharing their experiences with other schools in tackling these problems. Many countries are now seeking ways of ensuring that external assessments do not narrow or ossify learning developments, while continuing to provide valid evidence about the effectiveness of schools for accountability purposes. This quest is usually coupled with a concern to develop teachers' skills and confidence in assessment, in order to improve learning and enable teachers to play a much enhanced role in the development of their accountability function.

These examples reveal rather contradictory conclusions about the systemic reform endeavour. On the one hand, they reinforce the idea of the inter-connectedness of the different elements. On the other, some would argue that the dominant metaphor used in proposals for systemic reform is mechanistic, relatively static and linear. It owes too much to images of machines and of self-regulating systems drawn from the industrial production models. These characteristics mean that, despite its strengths, such proposals do not capture the complex nature of educational change. An alternative approach is to draw on organic metaphors from biological and ecological studies. These allow us to use a broader and more complex image of what has been described as a self-organising eco-system. This richer formulation is consistent with the idea that successful change in complex systems is evolutionary. It also underscores the notion that modern organisations depend on continuing learning by all concerned for growth, self-evaluation, development and productivity. Policy design and development can be gradually improved by working towards greater coherence between the various elements of reform programmes. This reduces ambiguity and provides a basis for more tightly targeted resource allocations and more focused interventions.

Policy design and development

One way of countering opposition to change while spreading costs is to adopt a longer horizon to reforms. This is also desirable because it allows for greater continuity and stability in programmes associated with improved educational outcomes. It allows more realistic time periods for implementation and for observable and measurable results to be realised. Electoral cycles are relatively short in most OECD countries and the length of ministerial office even shorter. The pace of public policy and social and economic change have also accelerated, forcing educational institutions to show that they are adapting themselves. It is unlikely that education reforms can be stretched over longer time cycles without some political realignment.

A traditional response has been to advocate bipartisanship around education policy. This has become less successful as democracies have become more pluralist and as social expenditure has increased. The emerging emphasis on *partnerships* as a means of harnessing intellectual and fiscal support may be one way of stabilising the reform process. Partnerships which share a vision of improved outcomes from education and improved productivity of schooling can strengthen the reform process by keeping a focus on the issues that really matter. Accordingly, policy-makers need to invest more time in fostering partnerships. Further, a common failing in policies is the disjunction between design and implementation. This can be addressed and even overcome by involving those who will implement policies in the design phase by representation in teams, by piloting and field testing, and by consultation.

The nature of reform also needs attention. Enthusiasm for change can be out of step with the nature of the education production process, which benefits from stability and continuity. If it can be assumed that the broad policy settings are right, more attention can be focused on improvement at the institutional level, on teaching and learning which are at the heart of the matter. Reforms usually have to work through many intervening variables via diffuse and often weak inter-relationships. Avoiding assumptions about simple cause and effect relationships, where these do not exist, would save valuable resources. It would also avoid overselling the likely outcomes of reforms.

The impact of evaluation has continued to be uncertain over the past twenty years or so, even though many expert teams are now at work. While the craft of evaluation has improved significantly and monitoring systems have become much more effective, there has been relatively little impact on policy-makers. The short time-lines of policy-making, and the overstated objectives of some reforms, have precluded a substantial formative role for evaluation. Nevertheless, it is clear that to build evaluation expertise into the design phase can help clarify objectives and the milestones for realising outcomes. Evaluation ought to be a necessary arm of policy implementation.

Pointers for the future

The findings and issues emerging from the Teachers and Curriculum Reform in Basic Schooling and related OECD activities suggest areas for further inquiry and investigation. Many of these are congruent with the lifelong learning priority, as well as other suggestions for further work, contained in the communiqué issued after the 1996 OECD Ministers of Education meeting.

Despite all the attention to and rhetoric of reform of the past two decades or more, it is most striking that school practice remains so stable, and the classroom relatively impervious to change. This in itself suggests further questions for research and enquiry. Yet, the study also illustrates that some innovative reforms in subject-knowledge are leading to radical changes in the classroom and in the effectiveness of student learning.

The notion of system-wide control, and the gaps that exist between aims and implementation, help draw attention to a disparity between the way education and training systems are structured and how leading firms are organised. Despite some obvious differences, both firms and schools work within a culture of knowledge, organisational practices and use of personnel. These are areas where educators could identify practices from non-educational sectors that might bring about more effective educational reforms and management. Successful innovations could be analysed, involving the spread of new work practices and today's technological possibilities, so as to identify approaches for more productive and cost-effective educational reform.

Reforms have their origins at many levels in the system and cover many strategies. Each of the different actors involved can be involved in generating positive change, as reinforced by CERI's work on Innovations in Science, Mathematics and Technology Education (Black and Atkin, 1996), which has shown examples of successful innovation arising from within the school itself. The findings from that study and other OECD work confirm that educational reform should concentrate on the school and be focused on teachers, who are the key partners in any real change at school level. It should be based on a comprehensive understanding of what enhances student learning and of the full range of functions and responsibilities that schools fulfil.

For further consideration

Teaching and learning call for reform and renewal that exploit the benefits of active modes of learning and reflect the increased emphasis on co-operation, team-work and practical knowledge in modern workplaces. What are the implications of these innovations for the organisation of teachers' work, for the structure of formal institutions, for assessment and for standards-setting? What are the significant curriculum issues to be identified?

The tension between the image of the school as a production line with divisions of functions and degrees of specialisation needs to be squared with the economic and social demands for a more dynamic school that emphasises practical reasoning and community studies. How could the design of schools be modified to minimise this tension? Are there other designs and approaches that might increase the quality of learning?

Comparative information and qualitative analyses show the contextual relationships shaping and influencing best practices. Comparing existing studies and correlating findings across different cultures and settings could provide a richer base for decision-makers. This synthetic endeavour could return immediate benefits and provide a basis for more encompassing definitions and conceptual work.

2

CURRICULUM AND SOCIETY

DEFINING THE CURRICULUM

The basic notion

Usage of the term *curriculum* is subject to considerable variation, but here a broad interpretation is assumed. The curriculum is a field of enquiry and action on all that bears upon schooling, including content, teaching, learning and resources. The perception of five layers put forward by Goodlad (1979) is borne in mind:

- the *ideal curriculum* is defined by its developers;
- the *formal curriculum* is that which gains official approval from the state and school boards and is to be adopted by institutions and their teachers;
- the *perceived curriculum* is what parents and teachers believe to be the curriculum which will reflect their subjective views on what should be taught;
- the *operational curriculum* is what is presented to students in classrooms, which may differ yet again;
- the *experiential curriculum* is what is actually experienced by students.

Goodlad further notes three levels of decision-making about the curriculum:

- the *societal level* concerns those decisions made by persons or agencies removed in time and place from the individual learner such as boards of education and federal policy-makers;
- at *institutional level*, curriculum decisions are taken by principals, teachers and school committees;
- at the *instructional level*, individual teachers decide what shall be taught in settings under their own control.

These notions of *layers* and *levels* are useful in reminding us of the complexity of curriculum as a concept and in setting a context for general discussion. They cannot, however, be fully explored here. References to the three levels will arise as the practice in different countries is considered, but the layers will not be addressed systematically. The present purpose is to consider some underlying principles rather than to explore how decisions about the curriculum are made.

Content and structure

What are the determining factors in defining the curriculum? Economic development is dependent on providing the latest knowledge that leads to success in the global market place. It is tempting to suppose that education is, therefore, a matter of ensuring high achievement in academic disciplines for all students, a case of becoming smart rather than becoming good (Lickona, 1993). But as Dewey has argued, the distinction is a false one. Education has no end but itself. Acquiring knowledge and understanding is a virtuous activity through which we become good. In short, education is a moral enterprise entirely concerned with the development of the mind. To stress technical achievement for its own sake is a distortion that takes the school closer to training than education.

Such views have been revived by post-modernist writers. Pinar *et al.* (1995), for example, suggest that the curriculum exists not to produce accomplished test-takers and high scorers nor to produce docile employees, but to help the young think and act with intelligence, sensitivity and courage in caring for themselves and others as citizens in democratic societies. The weight given to these varying views will depend upon a country's social and economic priorities. Where both are seen as important, emphasis may be given not only to the acquisition of knowledge but also to the way students are encouraged to organise, analyse, and indeed criticise, its structure, and the way it is used. The *Finnish* curriculum framework illustrates this approach. While recognising the growth of knowledge, it notes that students should understand how it is derived and selected and recognise its structure and validity. Students should learn how to adapt knowledge to fit the problems they are solving and organise their own structure of knowledge. In a similar fashion, the *Spanish* curriculum has content grouped around fields or areas of experience: concepts; mental schemata and a world-view; procedures or skills; attitudes and values; and moral development.

The sources of content again reflect a country's priorities and traditions. In *Norway*, three are identified:

- *experience-based knowledge*, derived from practical work and experiential learning. The purpose of content is to convey how living standards have improved by chance or design. There is an element of *tacit knowledge* in this formulation;

- *subject-based knowledge* in the study of languages, mathematics, social and natural sciences. This is essentially *propositional knowledge*, derived from evidence and research and tested by logic and fact;

- *cultural tradition*, displayed in the arts and crafts, in language and literature, and in theatre, music, dance and athletics.

Germany lists three sources of content:

- selected content from the *sciences* that fit the context of school subjects;
- *cross-curricular* tasks such as political and environmental studies;
- the student's need for *personal* development.

The *Portuguese* curriculum identifies five sources:

- scientific knowledge and its actualisation;
- cultural heritage – literature, history, philosophy;
- consideration of present-day social and economic issues;
- knowledge derived from learning by experience;
- consideration of society in a state of change.

The relevance of content to a student's perceptions will depend upon the styles of teaching and learning used, including emphasis on the application of knowledge. Content will also change as new knowledge arises. *Norway* encourages students not to perceive science as eternal truth but to apply a critical approach that will help them retain an open-minded view of new theories. The education institutes in the *German Länder* have developed tools to assist in assessing the need for curriculum change, including opinion polls for students, parents and teachers. The state is deemed responsible for school reform and curriculum development.

Coherence

Many countries give weight to the necessity of curriculum exhibiting *coherence*, though the term is easier to use than to define. A cross-curricular programme will derive coherence from its topic while bringing together a group of conventional subjects in an eclectic fashion. On the other hand, a course in combined sciences may give the appearance of coherence but in reality present each subject in a disjointed way. Certainly, however, coherence will bear a close relation to the way in which the curriculum is structured.

Most curricula are formed from conventional academic subjects. According to Walker (1990), traditional subjects "have become so familiar for so many generations that they might tend to seem more works of nature than of humanity". It is easy to take a narrow view of subjects but these can be reconceptualised as new content reveals ways of absorbing old content in more insightful ways. Teachers' familiarity with subjects can help promote coherence. There does not have to be a conflict between teaching subjects in their own right and using subjects in an interdisciplinary way. Thematic approaches offer students valuable interpretations of the world around them and can arouse interest in the specialist pursuit of subject knowledge.

Norway safeguards coherence and continuity in a core curriculum based on progression, subject differentiation and common topics for all students. A few subjects, like the national language, are taught throughout schooling. Some topics, such as civics, are split among several subjects as students move up to higher grades. Some, such as English, are begun at different stages. Some can be completed before the final year. The curriculum also supplies scope for the pursuit of local issues. A municipality may suggest priority topics and indicate appropriate guidelines.

The Netherlands requires schools to prepare their own curriculum design consistent with the national guidelines. The primary school is expected to have a "well-balanced curriculum" geared to each individual's needs and the diverse demands of the surrounding environment. Legislation lists the broad fields of knowledge that should be addressed and indicates how they may be structured as subjects without necessarily demanding adherence to them. However, core objectives have been established for each field and schools are required to use them, for example by using recommended textbooks. At the secondary level, for students aged from 12 to 15, a core curriculum of 15 subjects has existed since 1993, each linked to attainment targets: English; French or German; mathematics; physics and chemistry; biology; home economics/health education; history and civics; geography; economics; technology education; information science. Two subjects may be chosen from the visual arts, music, dance/drama and physical education.

Cross-curricular approaches

Other countries place emphasis on interdisciplinary work within the defined curriculum. This can be conducted at three levels:

- *cross-curricular* activities identified for consistent treatment in some or all subjects. Communication and numeracy are obvious candidates. Problem-solving and learning how to learn are other possibilities;

- *activities added* to the normal timetable outside subject boundaries. A project might be introduced that requires ideas to be taken from special subjects and used in combinations. The topic becomes the steering device for the curriculum element;

- *more radically*, the curriculum structure may include integrated elements that transcend subject boundaries in order to serve new societal aims or student interests.

In the latter case, the structure might make use of broad areas of enquiry such as mathematics and science, humanities, performing arts and so on. Within these areas, learning might be arranged around some organising principle such as that of narrative. Timetables are divided in Sweden into subjects, but schools are urged to develop interdisciplinary teaching around themes or problems derived from current realities. The core curriculum in Finland invites schools to make use of a series of topics as the basis for cross-curriculum studies, including international, consumer, traffic, health, media and environmental education, information technology skills and entrepreneurship. A similar approach in *Spain* offers topics on civics, moral concerns, sex and health, environment, gender equality, road safety, peace and consumership. In the *Czech Republic*, a number of cross-curricular topics are listed for inclusion in the basic curriculum. The recent addition of sex education has been controversial since the subject had previously been dealt with as part of biology and physical education. Developments such as HIV prevention have led to demands for its explicit inclusion. Several competitive proposals for the project were considered, with public discussion invited and the Ministry of Education monitoring the project through an interdisciplinary team. Adoption of the project is now a matter for individual schools.

INCLUSIVITY

Widening of opportunity

Since World War II, educational change in most Western democracies has been promoted by the state so as to provide greater equality of opportunity for its citizens. By means of a centrally-prescribed curriculum and more inclusive or "comprehensive" forms of schooling, central policy-making has been directed towards developing schools which will play a major part in mediating students' futures in society, and thus determining their access to its goods and rewards. Equality of opportunity for success in labour markets, stemming from the requirements of relatively large industries and services organised as command and control systems, has been the chief aim of public schooling.

In some countries, such as the *United Kingdom*, equality of social opportunity has been pursued by attempting to raise school standards, defined conventionally as success in academic subjects in line with university programmes. The maximisation of access to higher education has in effect become the major function of post-war schooling. In other countries, such as *Austria*, dual vocational and academic systems have developed as a way of maximising opportunities for all students on the assumption that the two systems enjoy parity of esteem. Sustaining equal opportunities by gender has become a concern in many countries. *Austrian* statistics show that girls continue, despite the provision of special programmes, to opt for different kinds of education than boys, selecting careers in social, education, business- and language-oriented fields, while boys are drawn to science, technical studies and economics. When choosing apprenticeships, 60 per cent of girls opt for one of the three occupations of shop assistant, hairdresser and secretary (Austria, 1994a). Currently, discussion is proceeding on whether separate lessons for boys and girls can, paradoxically, be a means of ensuring a more equal distribution of preferences. In Vienna, a private girls' school was founded in 1991.

Countries tend to set high academic standards for all students, but there will always be a gap between the ideal and the reality, which can be surprisingly wide. In the *Flemish Community of Belgium* a survey showed 13 per cent of all schoolchildren to be one or more years behind their peers when they finished elementary education. At the secondary level, the proportion can be as high as 40 per cent by the end of schooling. Children from low-skilled families are usually more affected by learning difficulties and may require additional resources. Greater attention is being paid to the role of "psycho-medical centres", which have a complementary role in the counselling, study and career guidance of students. The centres operate in teams, comprising psychologists, educationalists, social workers, physicians and paramedics. They are expected to play a more active role in dealing with problems associated with drugs, truancy, and personal relationships, co-operating closely with schools and other authorities and focusing more closely on low achievers.

Apart from social and moral considerations, failure to deal equitably with a nation's youth can have severe economic effects. Education is an essential part of economic and labour market policies. The OECD *Jobs Study* (OECD, 1994), whose purpose was to determine the causes of unemployment and find solutions, noted that equity in education is essential, if lifelong learning is to be realised, with the means of upgrading skills and jobs. Low achievers in school go on to form the greater part of the unemployed.

The pluralistic society

The curriculum exists to support and fulfil the abilities of all children. The principle of equity is therefore of salient importance in OECD countries and profoundly influences curriculum decisions. Equity also underpins the concern about racism, discrimination and intolerance. Dealing with diversity – the social, ethnic and gender differences among students – requires reconciliation between general objectives for all students and the need to differentiate for individuals in organising teaching and learning. This is a significant factor in increasing the complexity of the teaching task. Where many schools could once regard their students as monocultural in background and relatively homogeneous in ability, a classroom now may well contain students of varied abilities and from several different cultures.

In the *Netherlands*, the great variety of cultures is ever increasing. It is often unclear which languages are involved and what status they may have for the individual. The official position may be described as a compromise between assimilation and pluralism, that is, integration but with maintenance of the culture. Dutch prevails as the general language for teaching, but immigrant and non-Dutch-speaking students receive special lessons in Dutch as a second language until they are able to attend regular lessons. Two groups of children are taught in their mother tongue: those in schools established mainly for the children of visiting professionals, such as diplomats; refugee children from the former Yugoslavia so that they can be prepared to return eventually to their own country. The national constitution includes two articles dealing directly with cultural issues. Article 1 forbids discrimination with respect to religion, philosophy of life, political conviction, sex and race. Article 23 establishes freedom of education, thus reducing the influence of the central authority over the curriculum and permitting parents under certain conditions to found and organise a public or private school that meets their own pedagogical or religious requirements. One unexpected consequence of this is that the variety of cultures represented in a public school may be reduced. In recent years, the development of schools catering exclusively for particular ethnic minorities has been discouraged. Multicultural education is designed to contribute to a harmonious and pluralist society pursuing three aims:

- education should offer insights into the ways in which values, norms, customs and contexts influence human conduct;
- groups with different ethnic or cultural identities should learn how to live together;
- prejudice based on ethnic or cultural difference should be prevented.

These provisions have led to a debate between the "multiculturals" who want different ethnic groups to live together harmoniously and the "anti-racists" who lay stress on the structurally weak position of some ethnic minority groups and seek greater recognition for them in their own right. Of late, the two positions have moved much closer together. Teachers are advised to see each child as an individual with a unique and changing cultural character rather than as a member of an ethnic group defined by certain characteristics.

In Finland, on the other hand, the population is virtually monocultural, though there is a small immigrant mix. Schools are encouraged to use the experience and culture of immigrants as a source of enrichment. At the other extreme, the colonial heritage of Portugal means that many students will come to school unfamiliar with the prevailing language and culture. The curriculum strategies used to help schools respond to this diversity include: providing concrete learning situations that are related to previous cultural experience; using learning modes more sympathetic to the cultural experience of the student, such as stories and folklore; developing programmes for promoting tolerance and dialogue among different ethnic groups and cultures, which is the responsibility of a special department under the Ministry of Education. In Austria, "intercultural learning" as an interdisciplinary activity has been adopted as a teaching principle since 1993. Students are expected to learn, understand and respect linguistic and ethnic diversity, deal critically with ethnocentrism, Eurocentrism, and racial prejudice, and take an interest in other cultures. These innovations are of growing importance as new immigrants arrive from former Eastern Bloc countries and the former Yugoslav republic. In Scotland, intercultural issues are usually dealt with under the heading of "multicultural education" and may be linked with anti-racism and bilingual provision. Within the programme for 5- to 14-year-olds multicultural education is seen as a cross-curricular issue reflecting the many experiences of ethnic, linguistic and religious communities. All schools aim to provide the basis for a more rewarding and equitable society.

Minority languages which are intrinsic to a national culture also raise issues of equity. In Norway, for example, the curriculum must convey the common heritage, deepening the learner's familiarity with national and local traditions while recognising the international culture of minority groups. Thus steps are taken to safeguard the Sami language, whereby Norwegian students of Sami origin can choose to be taught Sami as their first or second language, an option also open to Norwegian-speaking children. The tension between heritage issues and the pressure for internationalisation has to be reconciled in finding practical solutions. In Spain, the languages of Catalan, Euskera and Gallego have equal importance with Spanish. In the Basque country, for instance, some schools develop the official curriculum in their own language and regard Spanish as a separate curriculum topic.

Special education

Children with special educational needs account for some 15-20 per cent of the school-aged population (Warnock, 1978). This means that every class of 30 children can expect to have some 5-6 students who have difficulty in learning at some time during their school lives. Some of these problems will be temporary but some will be more permanent. OECD countries in general have policies to integrate more and more children into mainstream schools from the special school sector. If these children are to be educated alongside their peers and be truly included, it means that teaching skills will be stretched to a maximum. There are implications for building design, classroom organisation, curriculum and pedagogy (see OECD/CERI, 1995c, 1995d, 1997b). Curriculum differentiation has become the main challenge. This involves designing teaching materials and methods which will allow all children – including those with special educational needs – to be learning skills which are part of the overall curriculum goals of the class and the whole school. This approach meets the challenge of special education, since it operationalises the idea that the problem of children with learning difficulties lies not within the child but in the school, the curriculum and the teaching methods adopted.

OECD countries vary considerably in the extent to which inclusion has been implemented, being widespread in Italy for example. In others, such as Austria, there are relatively recent reforms which are aimed at increasing the numbers of children educated in mainstream schools who previously would have been educated in special schools. In 1993, after comprehensive pilot projects had been completed, a legal basis was established for the enrolment of children with special educational needs in grades 1 to 4 of primary schools, and for the development of an integrated approach to the curriculum. Currently, several different models are being realised, depending on location and situation. In integrated classes, two teachers operate as a team and care for an average of 4 or 5 handicapped children. In co-operative classes, children of regular and special classes are taught together for particular subjects only. The auxiliary teachers provide special instruction, in addition to the regular curriculum, for up to 4 periods weekly for each child deemed eligible for special education training. In secondary schools, pilot projects are currently under way to establish the best conditions for teaching handicapped and non-handicapped students in an inclusive system.

The idea of curriculum differentiation, which as noted above is so central to effective teaching of children with special needs, is being increasingly developed through the identification of teaching objectives as expressed in individual education plans (OECD/CERI, 1997b). These provide the possibility to monitor progress on a formative basis, and this affords teachers the opportunity to modify their teaching and hence the curriculum to meet the needs of individual students. This approach is very valuable not only for those with special needs but also for all children in the class since it focuses on the teacher-student-task triad – a key component of successful teaching.

PRINCIPLES AND PRACTICE

Purposes and priorities

As indicated by the country examples already given, curriculum statements usually set out to embody, explicitly or implicitly, views about the purposes of education and its moral and social attributes. The starting point for such offerings, which must take account of the views of all concerned, is likely to be:

- continuation of the legacy of previous education documents, regulations and white papers – a distillation of democratic procedures and conclusions;
- persistent problems that are signals to society of the need for educational responses;
- the cultural heritage between tradition, the present and the future;
- developments in society at large: tensions will exist between current curriculum prescriptions and new perceptions.

In preparing statements of goals and directing subsequent actions, countries are usually guided by certain *principles* such as *equality* that are seen to be important. These may draw from any or all of the contributing fields of study – pedagogy, psychology, sociology and philosophy – and will also reflect political and religious considerations. In several countries values are acknowledged as essential. Social and moral education is concerned with fundamental issues of character. The personality of the teacher is of great importance in the character development of students. To make the point at its extreme, a computer programme can effectively teach important elements of mathematics but cannot contribute to the development of a student's capacity for moral judgement. Equally, responsibility for such matters cannot be left entirely to the school; co-operation between school and home is essential if the task is to be adequately met. In OECD countries, declarations of aims will be the result of these considerations and will form the basis of a curriculum prescription. The elements reflected will include:

- specific areas of knowledge and understanding, presented in broad frames of reference so as to provide progression, meaning and coherence;
- a common background of knowledge about democratic society;
- a respect for international issues as well as a country's own traditions;
- regard for lifelong learning;
- learning to understand oneself as an autonomous person.

Some examples follow with more detail of how particular countries have taken account of these elements.

Country examples

In *Belgium* (*Flemish Community*) the 1991 Government of Flanders Act for quality assurance distinguished three fundamental elements:

- *the content of study* has to do with what students are expected to learn;
- *supervision through inspection* is a way of monitoring what has been achieved;
- *support services* such as INSET and counselling address the issue of quality.

On content, the act stipulated minimum outcome standards for all schools, devised by the Department for Educational Development. To ensure that these were clear and widely supported a detailed procedure was followed. Departmental officials initially determined criteria by which objectives might be set, consulting teachers and principals in the process. Next, these proposals were made public for general debate by the Flemish Educational Council, representing all the groups concerned with educational matters. The Council finally made its recommendations to the government which, in turn, considered them before sending them to the Flemish parliament for ratification. The curriculum enunciates six guiding principles. First, it is important to control and sustain *narratives* as the young move through the school system. Continuity is specified as a sequence of attainment targets. Secondly, an emphasis on *active learning* stresses productive rather than reproductive tasks and a constructivist approach to learning. The curriculum design has been influenced by a shift of emphasis in the organisation of learning:

specialisation → general training
pure knowledge → applied knowledge

cognitive learning → broad education

planning by subjects → cross-curriculum education

sequential structure → theme-based education

short term training → long-term training.

A third principle is that of *horizontal coherence*: mutual relationships between areas of content at each stage are pursued, and overlaps avoided where possible. Fourthly, the principle of *intercultural education* focuses on learning and respecting other cultural value. Fifthly, *emancipatory education* seeks to promote equal opportunities for students of both sexes and from all social backgrounds. Finally, *limiting the study burden* aims to prevent individual subject content from becoming excessive and causing an imbalance within a curriculum composed of distinct subjects and levels.

The *Canadian* approach, in the province of Ontario, expresses its aims in terms of *literacies* (OECD, 1995b). The task is to build at each stage for all students an understanding in each subject area of reading, writing and problem-solving skills. The assumption is that almost everyone has the capacity to complete secondary school in terms of academic achievement, analytical skills and intellectual understanding. *Finland*'s aims for the comprehensive school require that students should become balanced, fit, responsible, independent, creative, co-operative, and peace-loving. The school must educate students in morality and good manners and give them the knowledge and skills necessary for adult life. It is important, too, to develop a student's readiness to learn and continue to learn, an affirmation of lifelong learning as an objective. The framework for the comprehensive school curriculum stresses that all solutions to human problems involve *value* judgements. The curriculum must convey values that strengthen individualism as well as those that develop or preserve society at large. Discussion of social and ethical problems is encouraged across the curriculum, drawing upon the values set out in the Declaration of Human Rights of the United Nations.

In *Germany*, the main curriculum goal should be the development of the student's own distinctive personality. The following cross-curricula objectives for each level were agreed at the 1995 National Syllabus Conference of the German *Länder*:

Nursery school – pre-school children should:

- know and understand forms of communication and the rules necessary when one lives in a group;

- find their way independently in familiar surroundings;

- defend their own rights by giving signals that can be accepted by others;

- be able to express their emotions within acceptable boundaries.

Primary school – children should be able to:

- deal confidently with a new assignment, showing patience in solving problems and coping with failure;
- supervise their own learning, possibly with guidance;
- lead by showing others what to do in a task situation;
- act discreetly by adopting an impartial attitude;
- admit they are wrong or powerless by apologising for mistakes.

Lower secondary school – students should:

- be able to compare learning or problem-solving methods with others, and draw conclusions;
- not immediately lose courage when problems occur;
- be willing to try different approaches to their learning;
- ask how they can be of service to others;
- express their opinions in different ways, depending on whom they are addressing;
- give others the right and freedom to hold another opinion.

Schools and school boards are free to enlarge upon these statements by means of their own school development plan and curriculum. On values, the constitution in Bavaria specifies: reverence for God; respect for religious convictions and human dignity; self-control; responsibility for one's actions; respect for truth, goodness and beauty; a sense of responsibility for nature and the environment. Students are to be taught in the spirit of democracy, affinity to their homeland and people, and mutual understanding and peace.

In the *Netherlands*, primary education is based on the following principles established in the Education Act:

- the education provided should promote the uninterrupted developmental process of children;
- it should be directed at the emotional and mental development, the idea of creativity, the acquisition of required knowledge, and improvement of social, cultural and physical skills;
- it should be based on the principle that children are growing up in a multi-cultural society.

All primary schools are obliged to design their own curriculum in the form of a survey of organisation and content over a period of eight years. General religious education of a non-denominational character is a compulsory requirement.

Norway recognises five principles governing the curriculum: equality, quality, continuity, participation and internationalisation. It cites seven dimensions to be fostered in students: the spiritual; the creative; the social; awareness of environment; the world of work; liberal education; the whole person. The aim is to build character and give students the capacity to take responsibility for themselves, make a commitment to society, and care for the environment. An explicit endeavour has been made to link the essence and spirit of various education acts, resulting in a core curriculum statement that aims to furnish students and adults with the tools they need to face the tasks of life, to qualify for participation in today's labour force, to prepare for new occupations, to develop specialised skills, and to assess the effect of their actions upon others. As in the other Nordic countries, the emphasis remains on Christianity as the source of moral belief. The core curriculum is centrally defined. Relevant guidelines are prepared for each level of schooling. At school level, teachers are responsible for organising the teaching and are required to produce a policy statement, the School Project, defining strategies, priorities and options, and the nature of links between the school and the community. A broad range of aims is specified: acquisition of knowledge and practical competences; promotion of global development; preparation for professional life; promotion of citizenship; development of an individual's potential; promotion of civic and moral education; development of autonomy and social responsibilities; provision of equal opportunities for all students.

The dominating principle in Portugal is the notion of education as a universal right (Portugal, 1993). All curriculum documents reflect the necessity of providing adequate cognitive methods and ensuring that learning should be student-centred. The Ministry of Education defines the core curriculum, the regulations and demands which are compulsory in every school. Typically, the curriculum includes general objectives for each cycle, specific objectives for each discipline or subject area, sequences of content and recommendations for practice, including pedagogical directions and suggestions for activities to be developed by teachers. At the school level, teachers are responsible for organisation and management with a certain degree of flexibility. Though Portugal is a mainly Catholic country, a tradition of secular education prevails, and ethical issues are presented in the curriculum from a non-religious perspective. The 1989 Education Act defines a cross-curriculum area of personal and social education to be implemented at four levels: in every curriculum area or discipline; in interdisciplinary enquiry based on projects and themes; in extra-curricula activities; in a separate curriculum element, termed "Personal and Social Development", that is offered as an alternative to the moral and religious education, chosen predominantly by Catholic students.

Spain has defined the basic elements of the curriculum as objectives, content, methodology, organisation and assessment criteria, which are established as broad statements of purpose by the Education Administration (Spain, 1994). It is accepted, however, that teachers and the community will mediate them and frame the curriculum in the light of their own particular contexts. Teachers and parents jointly prepare the School Educative Project, setting out aims, objectives and strategies for collaborative effort. Teachers, for their part, must formulate their agreed decisions on objectives, methods and assessment in the Stage Curriculum Project. Each classroom teacher must prepare a Classroom Programme, showing how learning experiences will be organised and adapted to meet the needs of all students. The curriculum has been criticised in the past for its emphasis on cognitive and intellectual abilities to the exclusion of other forms of achievement. The new curriculum seeks to promote five forms of development: cognitive and intellectual; physical and motor; personal and affective; interpersonal; social. This is to be achieved through the three elements of: content, facts, concepts and principles; procedures and rules; attitudes and values.

The Swedish Ministry of Education and Science, in The Inner Work of the School (Sweden, 1995), stresses the changing needs of students. Compared with earlier generations, the relation between the young and adults is seen to be more equal. Young people today learn about other countries and cultures at an earlier age. Education should respond to students' own observations and experiences while also taking account of the qualities that schooling should encourage. The curriculum should include: basic knowledge and skills; cognitive ability; interpersonal skills; collaborative working skills; motivational skills; a desire to achieve; a capacity to reflect upon one's own actions and the views of others. It should: contribute to the self-fulfilment of students; promote civic and moral education; evoke respect for diversity; encourage self-realisation, both personally and within the community; decentralise educational structures so as to stimulate decision-making abilities at the local level. The teaching of content is steered by goals set out in the curriculum and syllabuses. A distinction is made between goals for the activity itself and those related to the process or the way the work is to be carried out. The new curriculum materials establish the former but not the latter. Each school is required to determine its own teaching goals and decide with students how they can be met. In this way, national goals are meant to be interpreted at the local level.

Resources for learning

Textbooks continue to be the predominant learning resource in most countries, despite the advent of instructional technology and substantial resources devoted to the provision of computers. The way textbooks, and books in general, are used depends on the character of the engagement between teacher and learner. Books no longer have an exclusive place in the repertory of learning aids. Some countries examine published texts and prescribe those recommended for use in schools. Others, as in the Netherlands, rely on a government agency to review textbooks and publish a "consumer guide" to assist teachers in making choices. In the *Czech Republic*, textbooks have traditionally played a dominant role. New texts are now appearing, linked to the reformulated curriculum. A teachers' newspaper publishes details of new proposals or documents, reviews new materials, and offers a forum for the exchange of ideas on practice. The media provide an additional teaching resource; for example, the Ministry of Education has an agreement with the public broadcasting service. Interaction between the school and the world outside is seen as a valuable resource for learning.

The use of information technology in schools seems now to have come of age, as the hardware becomes cheaper and more flexible and students themselves become familiar with its use through toys and games. Teachers are enabled to act as facilitators, mentors and companions in the learning process, since they are no longer the sole source of accessible knowledge. The Internet and electronic mail allow schoolchildren to take part in projects shared with other countries. Technology influences the school in a number of ways:

- content can be addressed more informally, allowing students to focus on ways to have access to information;
- turning information into knowledge means that students must learn how to manage and structure it;
- as new technology becomes a part of daily life, it is now a natural part of teaching and learning. It is both applied and discussed for its ethical implications;
- the status of the teacher is changed as he or she becomes less of an authority-figure and more of a facilitator;
- textbooks are less important as new resources become readily available;
- school architecture is becoming more amenable to new ways of organising teaching and learning.

In some *Australian* states, new schools have been designed and built with extensive use of instructional technology in mind. In the *United States*, the Edison Project, a privately-funded initiative that contracts for public schools, provides each student with the use of a computer in school and at home, so that easy communication between home and school is possible. In *Denmark*, a major effort is being made to introduce information technology into all schools and subjects. Experiments are under way with the provision of a laptop computer for every student in a class. CD-ROM material has been made available to all teachers in order to introduce information technology into the classroom. The Ministry of Education has emphasised, however, that since computers cannot replace social and intellectual interaction between teacher and students, the tradition of classroom dialogue must be upheld.

School: a learning community

Formal school education arranges activities and encounters intended to foster positive learning outcomes. A number of choices arises when this task is operationalised: direct or indirect teaching; an orientation towards subject matter or students; adaptation for all children or focused on some conjectural average; focusing on individual development or the achievement of results; an emphasis on product or process. Teaching is the promotion, not the transmission, of learning. Much learning is unstructured and adventitious at home, at play, and even at school. What parents look for in a school is a structured environment where their children become educated. The European term *didactics* is used in several OECD countries to describe enquiries concerning teaching, learning and the curriculum. Its study may be pursued at the general level of aims of schooling, at levels of education such as pre-school education, and at the subject level. Elsewhere, these issues are considered to lie in the realm of curriculum and pedagogy and the term *didactics* is not in general use. In both cases, study will involve an eclectic consideration of particular problems in the light of the contributory disciplines of education.

Some individual examples will illustrate the variety of approaches. In *Norway*, the pedagogic task of the school is to view the child as a social, creative and spiritual human being in order that education can deal with personal qualities as well as subject matter. Learners from the first day of schooling are given duties and responsibilities so as to stress social learning and participation in the community. The *Flemish Community* has a similar pedagogic emphasis but expressed through the framework of defined attainments, which go beyond subject knowledge to such issues as environmental care and democratic behaviour. In most countries, there is a tendency to stress individual development and personal responsibility rather than group membership. Adaptive teaching respects individual differences among schoolchildren and is a starting point for exploring their knowledge, skills and experiences. In *Germany*, ideas stemming from the work of Montessori at the beginning of the century are experiencing a revival, and hands-on, independent, cross-curricula studies are receiving more attention. In the *Netherlands*, adaptive teaching is interpreted as giving each child a unique educational programme. Provision for children with special needs is increasingly offered in ordinary schools. A similar concern with child-centred education characterises *Spanish* primary education.

Pre-school education was a special concern of the report *Education for Europeans: Towards the Learning Society* (Cornelis, 1994), sponsored by the European Round Table of Industrialists. The document suggests that educational provision should begin well before the start of primary school, and notes the link between a poor socio-economic background and an absence of pre-school provision. Research indicates that exclusion from good jobs in adult life can be correlated with lack of pre-schooling and parental training in social skills. It is recommended that all children in Europe should have access to pre-schooling as part of the normal education system.

In *Austria*, compulsory schooling begins at age 6 but a pre-primary stage is provided for those of school age not yet ready for formal schooling. The *Czech Republic* has the same starting age, preceded by an extensive pre-school provision which has existed since 1948 and was originally related to the high rates of female employment. Currently, some 87 per cent of children receive pre-schooling. Some kindergartens have whole-day programmes. The curriculum now places a greater emphasis on the individual child and includes special programmes such as foreign languages, compensatory activities, and provision for gifted children. In the *Netherlands*, schooling is technically compulsory at age 5, but most children attend from age 4. The integration of infant and primary schools a few years ago provoked much debate about pedagogy for young children, with the result that the expertise of infant school teachers has become influential in teaching methodology in the new primary school. In *Spain*, infant education has been given special importance. The period from birth to age 6 is seen as an "educative stage" and there is a state commitment to provide resources for its development.

In the *Flemish Community*, nursery education dates from 1827 when it was decided to include children aged 3 to 5 in the education system and the first nursery schools were established. Currently, many children start school at 2½ and enrolment from age 3 is well over 90 per cent. Since formal school begins at age 6, a compulsory pre-school curriculum cannot be prescribed. Instead, "development aims" have been established and teachers use these as guidelines to adapt to individual children. In primary and secondary education, the nature of learning is so complex that the specialist categories upon which researchers focus may tend to obscure rather than clarify. Certain teachers find it difficult to combine increasing classroom demands with detailed study of the growing volume of research papers. As Bruner (1990) has pointed out, there is a danger that the current focus in psychology on information processing may distract educators from the brain's deeper function as a creator of meaning.

The concept of *active learning* has already been mentioned. In *Finland*, this is seen as a constructivist rather than behaviourist notion. The teacher's role changes from that of a disseminator of information and knowledge to a mentor who plans the learning process and its environment. *Norway*, likewise, aims to develop the students' sense of enterprise and desire to learn. The teacher is encouraged to use a wide range of methods and forms of activity. The core curriculum also stresses *creative learning*, thereby encouraging a student's natural inquisitiveness and capacity for divergent thinking. Education provides both factual insights and practical skills designed to develop "both head and hand". Increasing attention is being paid in several countries to the dimension of *social learning*. This will normally include development of social responsibility through making decisions with consequences for others; experience of working with others and developing leadership, and the ability to collaborate on tasks; learning experiences drawn from the school community, so that personal problems can be viewed in a wider perspective and conflicts defined and resolved.

In *Belgium (Flemish Community)*, the objectives for social skills are threefold: mastering a wide spectrum of interpersonal behaviour patterns; mastering mutual communication; working with others in an organised way. In addition, students are expected to acquire a sense of public responsibility by finding solutions to problems involving their peers and seeing how to carry them out. Thus, health education will lead to knowledge of how to use stimulants and medicaments for one's own good and that of others, and the need to regulate one's own conduct. Environmental education tackles issues such as water and air quality, noise pollution, and the need to act in service of others. A tendency evident in several countries is that of linking the school curriculum to some concept of *generic knowledge*, often not explicitly stated. For example, the "Thinking Skills" programmes prominent in the *United States* in the 1990s aimed to provide students with forms of knowledge that would equip them to tackle a variety of problems. For that matter, the growing use of the term "skill" within the last twenty years indicates a belief that much school knowledge can be freed from particular contexts and deployed through generic capacity. It is not clear, however, that high-level skills can be regarded as free from their context.

During the 1960s, talk of encouraging children to *learn how to learn* prefigured these later developments. The concept still has a prominent place in much thinking about teaching and learning, an example being in the new *Flemish* curriculum as an emphasis on the process and development of learning and study methods from primary school up to the end of the first secondary cycle. Students are encouraged to use different sources of information, and be able to assimilate it coherently by examining its content and structure. A tension exists, of course, between the care educationists express for the conduct of the learning process and parents' expectations of judging education in terms of its results. Achievement and performance have become more prominent measures of school quality than ever before. There is a danger that a concern for emphasising outcomes may lead to less concern for designing education processes primarily for individual development. Some believe that satisfying both demands is an impossible mission. Others would argue that the concept of quality in education can be reconceptualised so as to render the *tension* a source for continuous improvement and innovation. This is discussed further in the section on assessment.

CHANGING SOCIETY, CHANGING NEEDS

Impact of change

The OECD report, *The Curriculum Redefined: Schooling for the 21st Century* (OECD/ CERI, 1994), outlines a basis for curriculum reform, emphasising the rapidly changing social context, the place of individuals in schooling, the goal of lifelong learning, and the difficulties that arise in the course of implementation. It is generally encouraging that reform is possible in societies that both recognise an urgent need, and secure popular support for it. A central problem in extensive policy reformulation for schools systems is the long timescale involved. Schools seem unable to respond rapidly to radical innovation, since it takes time for teachers to adjust and to become confident of the changes being proposed. Attempts to force the pace may encounter considerable inertia or even opposition, both overt and covert, and little effective transformation is to be expected in the classroom. It is also far from easy to postulate the shape and content of new educational programmes. Some curricula exclude certain students, whereas others make special efforts to deal with the entire range of abilities. At root, schools are faced with a range of decisions from responses to such societal ambitions as diversity and active learning and to the pressure for good standards and new forms of assessment.

All the time the population is changing in structure, and rates of participation in education keep going up, patterns of control and administration are reformulated, and new insights emerge as the community becomes broader in scope and purpose. The result is a tendency for countries to look afresh at their entire systems of education. In Japan, for instance, a 1994 ministerial report recognises the achievements of primary and secondary education, but identifies a number of problems, such as excessive competition, bullying, school refusal, and too little attention in the subjects studied to the natural environment. Japan is also experiencing profound social changes, such as an ageing population, a more information-oriented society, and a growing international awareness. The report urges education to return to the underlying goal of placing high value on the individual in society, and calls for co-ordinated efforts between central government, local authorities and schools.

There is also today an international perspective emphasising the need for students to acquire a generalised body of knowledge, skills and attitudes that, in Wielemans's view (1995), is "free of context and exchangeable". In Norway, the new curriculum seeks to promote the global dimension and recognises several key tasks:

- combining technical know-how with human insight;

- developing a highly qualified, versatile workforce;

- combining an international outlook with respect for national traditions;

- making it possible for Norway to exert international influence in two domains: promoting the common welfare of the world and protecting its environment.

The changing role of school

Arguably the allocative role of schooling, which assumes a stable work environment and a definition of opportunity in terms of concrete bodies of knowledge, is breaking down and cannot be recovered. Some have suggested that in European democratic societies, profound and irreversible changes are heralding a shift from modernity, based on science-like propositions about social conduct, to what is termed *post-modernity* (Doll, 1993). At the economic level, the globalisation of industry, services and communications is seen as an aspect of this shift, giving rise to businesses that are less hierarchical and more flexible; small federated units respond more readily to changes in an unpredictable market. Skilled people in the crafts and the professions will sell what Handy (1989) terms their *portfolio*, their bundle of capacities and talents, on a temporary and contractual basis to one or more organisations at any one time. Through lifelong learning, "portfolio people" will reconstruct their offering, learning new skills as old ones become redundant. On this view, unemployment will be a structural property of post-modern society in the next century.

The implication for schooling is that young people must be prepared for lives in which personal fulfilment is derived less from job satisfaction and more from participation as active citizens capable of changing the social conditions that define their identities. Post-modernists argue that cultural and ethnic diversity, along with the decline of stable jobs and careers, are already threatening to destabilise the post-war mission of educational policy. Equality of opportunity becomes a more complex pursuit if people no longer share a common view of the objectives to be sought. As unemployment extends to university graduates, the definition of academic success as mastery of traditional bodies of knowledge looks increasingly untenable. The question arises whether schools can reorganise their curricula provision and organisational structures in forms that enable those students in danger of social exclusion to situate their learning experiences in positive visions of the future. It might be answered in the following terms:

- the primary function of schooling should be to enable students to take more control over the construction of their own society;

- the implication is that teaching should foster students' personal qualities as well as transmitting traditional bodies of knowledge;

- the curriculum should be reconstructed in a form that enables students to discover and realise their own talents, taking responsibility for their own personal development and meeting the demands of equity;

- school organisation should be grounded in respect for students' capacities to assume responsibility for their own learning, a student-centred rather than a subject-centred approach.

Strategies for school improvement and general effectiveness may often have started from a traditional subject range and the notion that the curriculum exists to offer future careers to students. This may well be a recipe for excluding many young people from mainstream society. For underpinning this approach is the conviction that what Schön (1983) termed *technical rationality* forms the best basis for curriculum planning and policy. Should technical rationality prevail, there is likely to be a reinforcement of barriers between subjects, an emphasis on content rather than values, and a utilitarian approach to curriculum aims and content. Standaert (1990) suggests that a more helpful paradigm is that of *technical-interactive rationality*, derived from the work of Habermas (see Weyns, 1990). The aim is to secure a mutual understanding of central as well as local decision-making, while acknowledging that both competition and specialisation are necessary in appropriate fields of judgement and enquiry. Such an approach, it is argued, will introduce valuable elements into the curriculum such as coherence among subjects and applied knowledge.

One does not have to be identified as a post-modernist in order to embark on reforms of this kind. Much of the recent agenda is to be found in the writings of John Dewey, whose reconstructionist approach to education foreshadowed an emphasis on encouraging students to shape their own learning and hence their own lives. Following the Dewey tradition, the shortcoming of technical rationality were early pointed out in the work of Schwab and McKeon at the University of Chicago in the 1960s (Reid, 1994); they advocated an Aristotelian approach based on practical reasoning in identifying and solving problems. The object here is not to espouse a particular approach but rather to indicate that a point has been reached where the adoption of another paradigm may be emerging. There is always room, of course, for some circumspection. However, given the persuasive influence of technical rationality as a tool for educational analysis in most OECD countries, it may be time to plead for a fresh strategy.

Lifelong learning

The issue of *lifelong learning* is demanding special attention. The school contributes a core curriculum as a necessary aspect of democracy, the task, as The *Curriculum Redefined* puts it, of "establishing publicly known and acknowledged agreements about the substance of universal schooling" (OECD/CERI, 1994). This implies a redefined pedagogy, constructive use of evaluation, and the achievement of quality as well as equality. One of the implications of lifelong learning is the need to link schooling with extended opportunities for learning in adult life (OECD, 1996). Thus in *Portugal* the system must "guarantee a second schooling opportunity to those who could not attend school in proper time (...) and to those who come again to the education system by reasons of professional need or cultural progression" (Portugal, 1993). The *Japanese* system places emphasis on lifelong learning for a society in which people can freely choose learning opportunities at any time in their lives (Japan, 1994). Its premise is that school education can no longer be seen as a self-contained process during which all required knowledge is meant to be acquired. Instead, it must develop those personal qualities and skills needed for independent and community life in an era of dramatic change. School education must redefine content to determine what is fundamental, stressing the willingness for all to learn independently.

Within the European Union there is a growing emphasis on internationalisation. The *Northern Ireland* and the *Scottish* Curriculum Councils stress the need for "Thinking European", and have published suggestions for integrating a European dimension into the curriculum. In Bavaria, "Europa" is the subject of one of the main cross-curriculum tasks. *Portugal* has fostered "European Clubs" in a number of schools. *Austria* has promoted inter-Europe co-operation on in-service teacher training (INSET), teacher supply, and other policy matters (see, for example, Scotland, 1992; Endt and Hooghoff, 1994; Rocha Trindade and Sobral Medes, 1993; Moravec, 1994). The general aim, today, is to see intellectual flexibility as the main object of education. The school of the next century might be characterised by such concepts as intrinsic motivation, becoming responsible for one's own learning, collaborative education, gaining acceptance of ideas and acting as a "stakeholder". All these aspects of schooling should ease a student's transition to a place in society as an autonomous agent, but to achieve such a transformation will require all the resources of the most determined of societies:

- basic schooling will become an inclusive activity. All young people, including those with special needs, will have access to equal opportunities;

- content will be derived not only from traditional subjects, but also from interdisciplinary treatment of really broad themes;

- the personal and social development of students will be a primary concern. The coherence of subjects will be considered in this light. Values and beliefs will come to the fore in pursuing education for citizenship;

- issues of power and autonomy will loom larger. A balance will be sought between the concerns of teachers and parents and the quality of the system as a whole;

- the nature of professional life is changing; so that education must prepare students for careers marked by volatility rather than stability;

- the profession of teacher will be greatly affected. Teaching to benefit all means an adaptive strategy in the classroom, which must be reflected in both pre-service and in-service teacher education.

Initiators of reform

Curriculum change can occur by chance or by design and at all levels in a school system. There are many agents of change, both local and national, and most governments have become active players. The complexity of society generates a range of difficult problems and the field of education can appear to offer at least some solutions. Schools benefit from this attention by gaining a higher profile, but pay the price with greater demand for accountability. Though remote from the classroom, central governments commonly find themselves extensively engaged in the content of education, as they define core curricula and attainment targets. Reform initiatives, however, are expensive and the return on investment is not guaranteed. Support structures are often stratified, making control and direction more difficult. Moreover, although governments recognise that education is an investment of paramount importance, it is a soft target when the economy declines. Curriculum specialists, whether from universities, colleges or school systems, may find themselves caught between the initiatives of central government and their desire to serve the interests of schools. The two are not always matched. Teachers are, in operational terms, the principal actors but they are not necessarily equipped to initiate reform. Change affects them and their careers and alters the character of their working lives. They are sometimes understandably cautious and often conservative towards new initiatives.

A variety of change agents can be found, such as industrialists, professional associations, other bodies or individuals within the community who share a concern for quality in education. Some examples follow of ways in which OECD countries have undertaken educational change. The first concerns reform in mathematics, which has attracted interest in many countries. In the *Netherlands*, primary school mathematics changed slowly but positively, driven by a coherent network of subject specialists at different levels. Initially influenced by the "New Math" movement, textbooks changed and so eventually did practice. INSET courses, and the continuing influence of the professional network on attainment targets in the *Dutch* national curriculum, gave added coherence to the movement. This collaborative model is currently the basis for a reform programme in the teaching of the Dutch language.

The same principle of collaboration underpins the role of the *Dutch* National Institute for Curriculum Development (SLO, 1994). Although a national body, its context is decentralised and arises from both government and school initiatives. The SLO aims to strengthen the problem-solving capabilities of schools by supporting school development and innovation. It co-operates with other bodies, such as educational guidance centres and denominational innovation centres, and is financed almost entirely by the state, even though only 40 per cent of SLO time are spent on government assignments. The SLO's target groups vary greatly from teachers to trainers and retrainers, to developers of classroom materials, and to principals and policy-makers. It is closely involved in the development of national proposals for basic schooling, although only in an advisory capacity. In its collaborative approach, the SLO is in line with the research evidence, concluding that widespread involvement is essential if curriculum innovation is to succeed. School participation, networking, in-service support, textbook revision, assessment reform, retraining school principals: all are necessary mechanisms for aligning these elements within a common programme.

In *Scotland*, the programme for children aged 5 to 14 is based on collaboration and engagement at all levels. In *Germany*, each *Land* has an educational institute for curriculum development, evaluation and pedagogy, generally under the direction of the Ministry of Education. In *Portugal*, the present curriculum reform programme for the whole system is based on ministerial decisions with the involvement of teachers and specialists, but also draws strength from local groups concerned with sharing experience of innovation, originating from previous research projects. A further source of influence arises from teacher conferences and publications.

Strategies for reform

For policy-makers, bringing about desired change in curriculum practice is complex and uncertain. Attempts to plan for change by defining learning in terms of finite competences fail to recognise that learning is only indirectly connected with teaching. Dewey noted that "collateral learning" occurs in an educational encounter regardless of what the teacher may set out to teach. Strategies, therefore, must acknowledge these contingent considerations, permitting a variety of classroom encounters and taking account of the views of all those who can influence the quality of learning in schools. Before embarking on reform, policy-makers need to address several questions:

- for whom is the curriculum intended?
- what is the division of responsibility among the various actors and what is the balance of power between national, regional and local authorities?
- what reforms in school organisation and teaching methods are called for?
- will reform require the revision of the school timetables?
- how are new forms of learning to be matched to formative and summative assessment so that the innovation enjoys the same status as what it replaces?
- how much time is required for teachers and students to accept and become familiar with innovations without disorientation or stress?
- how will reforms meet the needs of everyone concerned and deliver equal opportunities to all students?

The time factor is easily overlooked. The curriculum cannot go on accepting new content or processes without becoming overloaded, so if something new is added, something else must give way. This inevitably entails territorial difficulties which must be settled with care. The temptation to add new content in line with new knowledge or some new political priority should perhaps be resisted. Study and enquiry in depth are generally more rewarding than the superficial coverage of facts and opinion. Moreover, traditional ways of apportioning time in the school may limit the capacity for reform. A daily schedule of 45-minute periods restricts the extent to which open-ended problems and enquiry methods can be validly introduced and sustained.

In OECD countries a number of different strategies are used for engaging participants in the design and implementation of reform, ranging from top-down to bottom-up and including numerous intermediate patterns. A few examples will illustrate this variety. In Norway, an OECD report on education (OECD, 1990) led to a far-reaching 1992 reform programme. The aim was to equip the national school administration with more knowledge about how schools were being run, and to improve communications and relationships between the government and school authorities at the municipal and county levels. A major step was to reduce the size of the central administration: several departments were eliminated, and the implementation of national regulations was decentralised. This example shows that school reform may need to be preceded by reform of the role of government.

There is an echo of this in the Finnish report on new curriculum frameworks (Finland, 1994). This observes that the successful introduction of innovations requires a reduction in centralised administration and the delegation of greater decision-making powers to schools, encouraging them to collaborate more with surrounding interests. In Scotland, major policy changes in curriculum and assessment have been approached consensually, with teachers actively involved through consultation and development. Where attempts have been made by the authorities in England and Wales to by-pass teachers and impose change, parents and teachers have worked together, as in the case of national testing, to resist the imposition and develop their own approach. Recent developments in the devolution of management to schools have helped consolidate links between schools and parents. It is interesting to note that in Scotland, though not in England and Wales, the reluctance of parents to become involved in the minutiae of management has been recognised; budgetary matters are left to the headteacher and not to the school board.

In Ontario, Canada, four factors have emerged as important in improving learning and teaching in schools (Begin and Caplan, 1994):

- an alliance between the school and its community so that the responsibility for raising and educating the young is shared;

- the provision of early childhood education so as to maximise the potential of schooling for all children;

- the continuing professional development of teachers, the single most important factor in improving the quality of schooling;

- the use of computers and related technology to establish the relevance of formal schooling to the world outside the classroom and to help students learn to think in more creative and co-operative ways.

Reform in the *Czech Republic* was an unusual case. It brings, however, many of these points into sharp focus. In the past, the concept of curriculum policy was unknown and the term "curriculum" was itself little used. The prescribed curriculum was uniform and a directly-manipulative instrument, strongly oriented towards content and disciplines. The new 1990 reforms began with legislation repealing the Marxist ideology, broadening social studies and humanities, allowing alternative curriculum development, and cancelling the state monopoly in textbook publishing. In the following two years, the process of transformation was driven by bottom-up initiatives, including: critical discussion of the existing curriculum; comparative studies of curriculum in democratic countries; expert studies and reform proposals from various *ad hoc* groups; public discussions on reform, and individual initiatives by schools and teachers. The role of the administration was essentially passive during this phase, as the *Czech* school became a laboratory for curriculum reform. In due course, however, unexpected problems emerged:

- many schools were unprepared for autonomous action;

- curriculum diversity raised problems for transient students;

- dissolving the rigidly defined former curriculum left a loss of coherence;

- market-oriented competitiveness between schools, both public and private, led to populist tactics and a decline in quality.

A review of the whole reform process (Czech Republic, 1995*a*) identifies three general conclusions to be drawn from this remarkable exercise:

- broad and deep reform is necessary, for isolated or cosmetic changes cannot go far enough;

- the reform cannot proceed through administrative direction; since participation of all the actors is vital;

- although reform should be deep, it should also be gradual, with continual monitoring and tuning. The sustained support of bottom-up initiatives is of the greatest importance.

For further consideration

The conventional subject boundaries in the school curriculum reflect long-standing academic traditions, but are being displaced by cross-curricular approaches, and by increased attention to the applications of knowledge, in the search for greater inclusivity. How is the curriculum to be defined, and by whom, to safeguard issues of continuity and coherence and to ensure quality in the learning experience?

Lifelong learning for all has been widely adopted as a basic underlying educational objective, to accord with our rapidly changing society. If all are to develop a love of learning, and the skills to give effect to this throughout life, what are the implications for the school curriculum and the role of the school within the community?

Schools are slow to change, though the curriculum must continually evolve if it is to be responsive to the realities of the modern world. How can effective dialogue be developed and sustained between all who share responsibility for and are interested in the quality of the educational service – policy and decision-makers, academics, teacher educators, teachers, parents, students, industrialists and others?

3

ASSESSMENT: POLICY AND PRACTICE

BACKGROUND AND CONTEXT

Assessment practices can exert powerful influence on teaching, on the implemented curriculum and on school ethos and organisation. It follows that assessment policies should not be seen in isolation from policies for curriculum reform and teacher development. Moreover, as John Nisbet noted in *Curriculum Reform – Assessment in Question* (OECD/CERI, 1993) "assessment systems show a remarkable resistance to change". Any proposal for reform depends on changing public and professional attitudes and assumptions about the functions of examinations and the nature of ability. Furthermore, without successful professional development of teachers, changes in assessment policies are unlikely to be effective. While there are observable trends and comparable developments in assessment across many OECD countries, there is some diversity as cultural differences and other educational developments in those countries are reflected in the approaches adopted. One notable example of diversity is that whilst some countries regard external assessments as an essential feature of their education system, others (including some with a reputation for high quality in education) have resisted moves towards more external assessment.

During the 1960s and 1970s in many countries, traditional external assessment systems became less important. In part, this was due to the move towards universal secondary education, whereby selective end-of-primary tests became redundant, and towards comprehensive schools which opened upper secondary general education to the mass of students, making some regard end-of-secondary certificate examinations as less needed. In part, the lower profile of external assessment in those decades reflected an apparent lack of public concern about educational standards; it also demonstrated confidence in the work of teachers and schools which was later to be eroded by the perception that some schools were failing their students. Reforms of the public sector in general, associated with demands for greater accountability for performance and expenditure, were extended to education. The call for higher standards which began to gain weight at the end of the 1970s produced a demand for higher curriculum standards, especially in those countries which lacked national curricular frameworks. Systemic reform – where assessment is closely integrated with curriculum reform – was a by-product of this development. As public concern about standards grew, there was increased pressure for accountability in the sense that systems, schools and teachers were increasingly required to demonstrate that students were meeting standards. Externally set and marked tests are often considered more reliable for this purpose than internal tests by teachers.

In countries where there is little external testing as yet, there are moves towards national testing (at least of samples of students at key stages), for the purposes of monitoring compliance with national curriculum requirements and changes in performance levels over time. In some cases, international studies have been instrumental in stimulating concern about standards in comparison with those of other developed countries. The OECD/CERI programme, Indicators of Education Systems (INES), has led since 1992 to an influential annual publication *Education at a Glance* (OECD/CERI, 1997*a*). Developing beyond this at the present time (1998) is the large-scale OECD Programme for Producing Indicators of Student Achievement, PISA, for which international surveys of student achievement are being planned in reading, science, mathematics and use of information technology. Countries not yet affected by the move towards system accountability, but which are participating in studies such as the Third International Mathematics and Science Study (TIMSS) carried out by the International Association for the Evaluation of Educational Achievement, may yet be drawn into this process. These studies provide participating countries with a set of international benchmarks of student achievement in key subjects. When a country's results in key curriculum areas are shown to be adrift from these international benchmarks – as with mathematics and science in the *United States* in the 1970s – pressure mounts on the government to do something about it.

Thus, countries may be at different stages. It is important to view systemic reform within this perspective and against the assumptions – such as teacher competence to assess – which underpin policy initiatives. End-of-secondary examinations for university entrance have been a relatively constant feature in countries such as the *United Kingdom*, *France*, the *United States*, *Canada* and *Australia*, even where the educational systems have been subjected to major reforms, and where policies within federal systems sometimes vary across states. The balance between internal and external assessment for this purpose varies over time and across countries, and some countries have separate processes for upper-secondary certification and higher education selection. In all countries these end-of-secondary assessments represent a powerful tradition which influences assessment throughout secondary education, and even primary, in some systems. Being generally curriculum related, they may be seen as a conservative influence, reinforcing subject-specific curricula and inhibiting innovation both in curriculum and assessment. It is clear, however, that these assessments generally command public confidence – the phrase "gold-standard" is used in *England and Wales* – and serve as a useful reference for employers and higher education. Some countries have begun to diversify both the scope and form of these examinations. Where, traditionally, diversified secondary curricula exist, diversified assessment procedures exist alongside.

Competency-based approaches to assessment represent an important challenge to more traditional forms of testing and certification; they can widen access to further education for they recognise that learning takes place outside the formal educational system as well as within it. Assessment of competence emphasises outcomes rather than processes and is a useful complement to academic testing. In the context of mass higher education and lifelong learning, countries are looking for a means of bringing these two approaches closer together.

Standardised norm-referenced tests, weakly tied to the curriculum, have been a feature for many years of system accountability in several, mainly English-speaking countries, especially the United States. National standardised tests are spreading to other countries, not usually to replace traditional forms of curriculum-related assessment, but for use alongside them, often with the specific purpose of instructional improvement or curriculum adjustment. Where a national curriculum exists the national tests are usually closely based on it. In the United States, where standardised testing is a well-entrenched phenomenon, the tests are criticised as insufficiently valid, because they are not specifically curriculum related, and because of the negative effects they are perceived to have had on teaching methods. There, as in Canada and Australia, the move is towards more specific definitions of curricular standards, in connection with which new performance-based assessment methods are being developed.

In countries where there is no crisis of confidence in educational standards, teachers' assessments are generally trusted, often reflecting the higher status of teachers in those countries. However, the development of "assessment literacy" among teachers is becoming a matter of concern in many countries. It may well become one in those countries which have traditionally assumed that teachers were professionally competent to carry out this function, if concern about standards and equity in selection procedures grows, as it seems to be doing in Italy and Denmark.

There is firm evidence, across many subjects and across all countries, that the spread in achievement of students in any one age group is very wide: it is common to find that the bottom and the top percentiles can differ in their scores by 60 per cent. International testing programmes show that the ranges of performance within all countries are much greater than the range in the differences of mean scores between countries – yet it is these inter-country differences that seem to have the stronger hold on public attention. Moreover, the evidence also indicates that it may take average students on the order of seven years to improve their scores by the same amount as the range of scores in any one age group. It follows that there are students in all countries who at age 10 (say) have only a small chance, by the time they leave school six or seven years later, of reaching a level already grasped by the top 10 per cent of their 10-year-old peers.

Often, the students near the bottom of the ability range will be labelled as failures year after year, becoming school drop-outs and the unemployable youth in adult society. Streaming, setting, and making students repeat a year of schooling are all attempts to cope with this problem, but seem inevitably too crude to respond to widespread and diverse student-needs, while research evidence suggests that settled groups produce lower overall performance than mixed groups of comparable ability. Repetition of a school year following poor performance is common in a few countries, though in some of these, such as *Germany* and *France*, the incidence is falling.

These brief comments about the background assumptions and historical context of the assessment procedures are intended to set the scene for the more analytical sections which follow.

PURPOSES OF ASSESSMENT

Data on the learning of students is collected to serve several purposes, which can be grouped as follows:

a) Teachers and students need frequent information on student performance in order to identify progress in learning and to expose needs. To provide such information requires frequent assessment – often but not always informal – embedded in the process of instruction. This purpose is formative and diagnostic.

b) Teachers need feedback information in order to improve their own teaching, which can come from formative or summative student assessment.

c) Formative and summative assessment data can also be used in improving the work of a school. There has, however, to be a strategy for aggregating the data in relevant ways. Thus data which assess overall gains of a cohort from year to year in each subject could be valuable, related to other data about policies, resources, and management within the school.

d) School accountability is a function which overlaps with school improvement, but with evidence addressed to parents, public agencies and the general public. The monitoring required here may focus on two types of evidence – the implementation of any external curriculum and teaching guidelines, and the performance achieved by students in the learning expected of them.

e) Summative results for individual students are used in selection for the next stage of education and for employment. Such information may be needed in the transition from primary to secondary schools, and for access to tertiary education. The function is more critical if higher education is available only to a small proportion of students (or, if wider participation is possible, where institutions differ greatly in status and popularity) and where employment opportunities are limited. In some societies, schools are trusted to produce informal statements or certificates, whereas in others external tests are thought essential, with or without data supplied by teachers.

f) Governments sometimes see the need to monitor the performance of students in key areas, especially following the implementation of reforms, not for purposes of school accountability but to fine tune curriculum guidelines or to answer political questions about standards. In this context (as noted earlier) several OECD governments also participate in IEA (International Association for the Evaluation of Education Achievement) studies in order to benchmark their students' performances against those of other countries.

The first three of the purposes above are essentially formative, being concerned with internal feedback for improvement. These purposes may require the information to be detailed in relation to the needs to be met or actions to follow. By contrast, the remaining three require data on which to base an overall judgement, and are therefore summative; they may be used as a basis for national policy development. Summative data for students can be simple and sparse, as in a single test mark or grade, but the trend here is to give more meaningful and structured information, in the form of a profile of achievement or portfolio of work. For policy purposes, performance data can be gathered by testing all students or by sampling, as discussed further below. The information used to serve all six purposes may be provided from inside the school, or from outside through the use of test banks, test papers or less formal procedures. Both approaches may yield data for more than one purpose. Thus, teachers' data can be used for both formative and summative purposes, national test banks can be drawn upon to aid diagnosis within a teaching sequence, and results of external tests can be analysed to evaluate teaching programmes. The ways in which these various sources are balanced and interact are complex, often depending on national traditions and cultures.

Authority, responsibility, implementation

The distribution of control and responsibility for public education across the national, regional or state and local levels differs widely among OECD countries. Some federal systems such as *Canada* have no national education policy – education is a state or provincial responsibility. Unitary systems such as *France* and *Sweden* retain national control over curriculum and assessment, despite moves to decentralise decision-making. In *Australia*, a national perspective has emerged through collaboration among the states in developing a curriculum framework for grades 1-10, expressed in terms of learning outcomes. Certain countries, notably the United Kingdom and New Zealand, have recently reasserted national control of education through national assessment, combining a demand for more explicit accountability with a movement towards increased decentralisation and local decision-making.

The purposes and forms of assessment reflect, to a considerable degree, the systems of control over education, but are not wholly determined by them. Traditional certification systems continue to have an influence, and prestigious universities, professional bodies and employers may exercise national influence over assessment procedures and certification even in the absence of national political structures for education. The lingering influence of British GCE (General Certificate of Education) Advanced Levels in Canada and Australia, American and Japanese entrance examinations for the most prestigious private universities, and employers' standards for vocational training in Germany are all examples of this phenomenon.

Nevertheless, to understand the operation of assessment systems it is generally necessary to relate them to the articulation of levels of political control. Thus, countries with national curricula generally have national assessment systems which offer some measure of students' achievements of the learning goals embedded within the curriculum. The extent and scope of the assessment system and its modes of implementation – by external examination, by teacher-directed internal assessment or by a system of national inspection, or combination of these – are largely determined by the intensity of public pressure for accountability. Thus, although both Japan and the United Kingdom have national ministries of education and national curricula, their national assessment patterns differ considerably.

In England and Wales, where public and political concern about education standards is high, all students take national tests at ages 7, 11 and 14, and almost all take the General Certificate of Secondary Education examinations (GCSE) at age 16. GCSE and GCSE Advanced Level examinations (taken normally at age 18) are conducted by independent boards with permanent bureaucracies and teams of school and university teachers who are paid to set and mark these examinations. However, following public concern about standards of accuracy and comparability in these high-stakes examinations, the central government has also begun to exercise greater control over the procedures for setting, marking and monitoring. In Japan, where public confidence in education standards is high, assessment is carried out internally by teachers up to the external secondary leaving examination. National testing of samples of students at key stages is carried out every five years to assess achievement of learning goals in the context of curriculum reform.

Federal countries – even those without ministries of education – usually have some central agency which monitors student performance, at least in core subjects at key stages. In Canada, the Council of Ministers of Education (CMEC) carried out a national assessment of a sample of students in mathematics, reading, writing and science. The national equivalent organisation in *Germany* (KMK), monitors the comparability of standards of the *abitur* in the 16 *Länder* (states). Setting and marking of the *abitur* is left mainly to individual schools in most *German* states, though the states monitor compliance with state curricula and comparability of grade boundaries between schools and teachers. In the *United States*, national assessment has often been linked with federal educational initiatives. The Department of Education conducts a national assessment (The National Association for Educational Progress) on samples of students at both state and national levels, mainly using multiple-choice tests.

Neither *Canada* nor the *United States* has a national curriculum, so the curriculum-relatedness of the tests is limited. However, they serve the needs of national accountability when there is public concern about standards in basic education. When assessment is carried out for these purposes at one political level but responsibility for action is located at another, issues such as determining, funding and evaluating the necessary follow-through action can become difficult to resolve. In *Australia*, there have been only two examples of national assessment, both in numeracy and literacy of 10- and 14-year-olds, in 1975 for the national parliament and in 1980 for the Council of Federal and State Ministers. Current practice is for states to conduct their own state-wide assessments which are comparable in a general way as they are increasingly keyed to curriculum frameworks based on the national ones.

In *France*, *New Zealand*, the *United Kingdom* and *Sweden*, national responsibilities and assessment policies are more closely aligned, although the purposes of national tests differ from country to country. In *Sweden*, every student takes a national test, following which the mean and spread of results for each school is determined. The school, however, determines the grades awarded to individual students, taking into account both the external test results and their own teacher assessments. Thus comparability is maintained across schools whilst due recognition is given to the more extensive knowledge that schools have of their own students. In *France* and the *United Kingdom*, national testing related to the national curriculum has not replaced traditional end-of-secondary examinations (the *baccalauréat* and Advanced Levels), although these examinations, which have traditionally served for university selection, have had to adapt in response to a great expansion in upper secondary education.

The *baccalauréat* in *France* has developed a wide range of options, including technical and commercial routes. Over 50 per cent of all 18-year-olds now take it, with 80 per cent of students expected to do so by the year 2000. In the *United Kingdom*, Advanced Levels are taken by an increasing proportion of students but expansion of the numbers of students post-16 has led to the development of a variety of alternative courses. These are intended both to safeguard the Advanced-Level standard and to accommodate the needs of a wider range of students. In both countries enhanced participation has given rise to fears about falling standards and to the construction of national "league tables" of schools classified according to their students' performance.

There is growing recognition of the fact that, while national authorities set standards and evaluate and report on their achievement by students, only schools, teachers and, of course, the students themselves can effect improvement in performance. Politicians and some academic researchers tend to assume that assessment operationalises the curriculum. In reality, however, teachers – the key agents in bringing about change – may be encouraged and supported by assessment procedures or constrained in their efforts. Whether reporting of test results is in the context of pedagogic improvement (*France*) or school accountability (*United Kingdom*), the intended follow-up action is left mainly to the teachers and schools. This is especially true in *France* where whole student populations are tested at key stages and results are primarily intended for diagnostic use by teachers in their lesson planning. To divorce the tests from any suggestion of accountability, the *French* national tests are conducted at the beginning of the academic year so that they serve as baselines for the new teachers. Tests in other countries such as the *United Kingdom* may be used for diagnostic purposes but this is not their primary objective.

Process issues

Technical considerations indicate the possibilities and constraints for assessment policies, but in practice account has also to be taken of underlying values and conflicting constraints. Well-informed policy formulation will recognise the constraints and consider a wide range of possible methods, not just the traditional procedures; it will seek to fashion optimum solutions across the different and competing targets. It is, however, the underlying values which will determine the priorities to be assigned and the balance to be struck.

Standards

The design of assessment policies and of assessment methods is closely inter-related to the setting of national or local standards. Apart from their value in setting targets for all schools, statements of standards can help as a basis for communication: between teachers, in the same or different schools; between students, parents, and their teachers; between schools and the numerous agencies outside schools. The publication *Performance Standards in Education: In Search of Quality* (OECD, 1995a) gives a detailed account of how ten different countries have developed their interest in setting performance standards – most of them only in recent years. The methods used for setting standards are very varied, as are the links between standards and methods of assessment. For example, standards may be minimum criteria which all should master. Alternatively, they set out ideals on the assumption that any one student may achieve competence with only a fraction of them. The assessment implications of these two approaches are quite different.

There are several different ways in which standards may be expressed. There are subtle but important differences between statements which start *Students should be taught...* and those which say *Students should learn...* or *Students should know and be able to*. There are also differences between lengthy discursive statements which set out a general philosophy and brief sentences which read – intentionally – as if they were describing laws. In a country with federal control over education, national standards might use the general philosophy approach, because the function of standards can only be to secure consensus by their arguments. In a system with national control backed by legislation, the prescriptive form might appear to be more appropriate.

There is a related problem concerning the degree of detail with which standards should be specified. Very precise definition leads to lengthy documents and to constraint on teachers' flexibility in teaching methods. Insofar as teachers may be led to teach to all of the detailed targets separately one-by-one, this can also lead to an undesirable atomisation of learning. Matters could be made worse if sets of short test items also reflect an atomised approach, thereby pressing teachers to teach in the same way. Very broad definitions lead to statements which are open to interpretation at different levels of complexity according to the different potential of different students. However, such broad definitions might leave the precise definition of standards in the hands of those who set test questions. Thus the choices here have broader policy implications in relation to the degree of authority over curriculum implementation to be delegated to schools.

A key link between the specification of standards and their use in assessment is the choice of approach between criterion and norm referencing. These are not polar opposites – they are two aspects of every assessment. In relation to the feedback functions of assessment, a parent or a teacher may well find it helpful to know that a 10-year-old cannot perform confidently on a specific type of task (the criterion aspect), and that this is a task at which 80 per cent of the age group are competent (the norm aspect). However, for formative purposes, the outstanding priority is to identify individual needs at a level of detail, which calls for a criterion-based approach. It may also call for replacing performance reports which use marks or grades by verbal reports which explain the main characteristics and implications of a student's work. This is being attempted in schools in the *Czech Republic* and for the first two years of primary schooling in some parts of *Germany* – where the primary teachers are finding difficulty in changing their practice in this way. For summative purposes, the detail is inappropriate and there have to be rules about aggregation over criterion-based results. A highly aggregated result loses the advantage of meaningful interpretation that distinguishes criterion referencing, and the norm aspect can then be more important.

A relatively new development which raises these issues in a different context is the move to a competency-based curriculum. The emphasis here is on outcomes in discrete skills and competences, notably those concerned with literacy and communication, numeracy, study and the use of information technology. These may be developed within and distilled from a variety of academic and non-academic courses. They are directly relevant to those outcomes of learning, by whatever route, that are of central relevance to employers and to individuals in respect of the capacity to keep abreast of, and to operate effectively in, rapidly changing environments. Arguably the competency-based movement can open up access outside the formal education system, counter the traditionally excessive emphasis on academic learning, and create a system which is better matched to the needs of lifelong learning. It could also be a way to break open the constraints on accreditation in that new bodies, notably those involved in distance learning and in the in-house training of firms and professional bodies, so that they might achieve recognition for this new mode. In relation to the techniques of assessment, it is clearly committed to criterion-referenced testing with an analytic, even atomised, approach. It has, however, to contend with distinctive problems of validity: an assertion that someone has "acquired a skill" must imply that they will be willing and able to use it in any relevant context, but the nature and range of the evidence required to support such an assertion is problematic. This difficulty is relevant both to the design of any teaching programme and to the implementation of assessment.

Reliability

Any assessment is but a small sample of the performance of a candidate. The confidence which users can place in assessment results is always under threat because it is hard to ensure that this sample gives a fair representation. Some of the causes of unreliability, such as marker variations or misleading wording of questions, can be settled with care; others such as variation of the interpretation of standards between teachers or variations in a students' alertness from day to day are harder to overcome. The most severe problem for external written tests is that they can only sample a small range of the possible types and contexts of questions that constitute the domain of performance on which the test is meant to provide information. For example, the result of two hours' work on a small number of mathematics problems may not legitimately be generalised to report on "ability to tackle mathematics problems". Where students can be allowed to take a long time and can therefore use open ended and extended response questions, these problems become less severe, particularly if the written tests are supplemented by oral examinations. However, the degree of uncertainty involved in the different approaches to external testing is not readily determined, which might lead to public confidence being undermined.

Assessment by teachers of their own students can be based on far more extensive sampling, but faces other problems of variable standards, individual bias, and possible conflict between the teachers' formative and summative roles. Here again there is a need for careful investigation of reliability, and for development and trial of procedures to enhance this, particularly to ensure that different teachers work to common standards. The problems of teacher bias, and of pressures on teachers from their students, from parents, and from their school, are all threats against which a system of checking must provide safeguards. In some *Australian* states, where teachers' assessments have been compared with results of state tests on the same curricula and criteria, it has been found that teachers' estimates give a wider spread of performance than the external tests. *Flemish Belgium* found internal school results to be better predictors of success in higher education than either IQ or external achievement tests. The problems are taken further in the section "Teachers' roles in assessment" below.

Validity

The technical issue perhaps of greatest importance for assessment policy is that of validity. This can first be interpreted as the problem of ensuring that an assessment process or instrument measures what it is designed to measure, success in relation to one of the aims of the curriculum. Shifts in assessment thinking can be driven by the intention to reflect validly a curriculum trend. Nevertheless, valid methods reflecting real classroom situations or real situations of application are either impossible to replicate or very expensive. Consequently in practice, most external tests are some form of surrogate measures. Unfortunately, surrogates may not always be dependable, as when students' performances on real practical tasks are found not to correspond with their performances on paper and pencil surrogates of the same task.

Moreover, a broader interpretation of validity requires student-assessment policy to be appraised in the light of the uses to which the results of assessments may be put, and whether decisions based on these can be justified. Thus assessment data might be used to judge the effects a particular policy has on teachers' work, on the work of schools and the curriculum, and on the work and prospects of students. These are aspects that will be discussed further in "Reporting and accountability" below. For example, in some countries the practical capability of students in tackling realistic problems is seen as the distinctive feature of vocational education, whilst others try to emphasise its importance for all. One consequence of the different approaches is that the assessment needs are seen to be different, with assessment of practical skills and project work in the vocational area, rather than the more formal tests in the academic. In part this shift is driven by concern for consequential validity, and in this view the use will be considered in appraising the validity of the assessments.

The limited validity of short and inexpensive external tests is a serious problem. Valid inferences are simply not possible on many issues, as they use the results of tests necessarily composed of short items on very specific topics or issues addressed in isolation. Such tests cannot, for instance, address a student's capacity to produce extended prose, communicate orally, pursue an investigation of an open problem in science or in mathematics, or design a technological artefact. Yet it is these capacities which are often more relevant to future study and employment than those which short tests can mirror. Valid assessment of such activities is expensive, however, and has to be extended over many tasks and so over long periods, if the results are to be generalisable.

Relationships between formative and summative

The distinction between formative and summative assessment seems more important in some countries than in others. It is not necessarily a distinction between agencies, since both can be carried out by teachers. Whilst teachers must be directly involved in formative assessment, agencies outside the classroom can play a central role, as the *French* national initiative requiring national tests to be used by teachers for diagnostic purposes has shown. Neither is it a distinction as to methods or instruments of assessment – some methods can be used for both, although others will be more suitable for one or the other of the two. The essence of the distinction lies in their purposes: formative assessment is directed to improving learning, whereas summative is for reporting, whether on individuals or groups. Where the same methods are used for both, the interpretations of the results will differ according to the two purposes.

It may be important for two reasons to emphasise the distinction, particularly in discussions of policy. The first is that formative assessment is often used as simply another name to cover all teacher assessment. Whilst most teachers give tests, mark students' work and ask students questions, the empirical evidence is that very few actually design and use these methods to reveal individual needs and modify the learning approaches. For example, the formative value of a test given by a teacher at the end of work on a particular topic may be slight, inasmuch as it is too late to deal with any problems that are exposed – the work is over and something new will be started next time. One reason for weakness here is that assessment is given little attention in initial training courses, which focus instead on "methods which work" and on "survival in the classroom". The second reason follows from the first – studies of teachers' formative assessment practices in the *United States*, in the *United Kingdom* and in *France* have all shown that it is the aspect of teachers' assessment skills and procedures that is most in need of further research and development. This need will not be taken seriously unless the precise nature of, and need for, formative assessment are clearly grasped.

Manageability and cost

Manageability and cost are also technical issues, which are too easily overlooked when new plans are being formulated: the acceptability of a system and the efforts made to prepare teachers and recruit their support are clearly at issue. Novel testing regimes have sometimes been abandoned because of teacher protests over the extra work that was involved for them. In some cases new external tests, which emphasise their value to teachers and offer resources for training, have been successfully introduced. Testing can consume a significant proportion of an educational budget, a significant investment of public money that can only be supported in the light of cost-benefit analysis of the different strategies available. The extent to which different methods can promote higher standards of teaching and learning is important. A new approach will be more robust if it shows such benefits while simultaneously satisfying the certification and accountability purposes. There are broader comparisons at issue also, for example whether resource is better devoted to school inspections than to testing. A country might realistically devote resources entirely to teacher development, with spending on national assessments deferred. To introduce new methods of assessment without giving teachers the training necessary to understand and handle them is clearly wasteful.

Equity

The broad aims of social equity have been served in many societies by the setting of external standards and testing. Students from districts or schools with low status have the opportunity to show that they have achievement comparable with that obtained by students in more privileged situations. This point is of lesser consequence in societies where class and related social barriers are less evident. The effects of status here raise the issues of equity between institutions, in terms of the ways they are resourced and judged. In *Italy* experience suggests that teachers inflate grades in the absence of external test constraints, which implies that school performance cannot effectively contribute to social mobility. By contrast, *German* school-based results retain public credibility and it is assumed that the different *Länder* are equally effective in ensuring comparable grading across the country.

Another dimension of equity is the treatment given to students with very different types and levels of achievement. It is all too easy for an educational system to assume innate differences in students' "ability", an assumption which can inhibit efforts to engage with the particular problems of a sizeable proportion of individuals. There are, however, students with special learning difficulties for whom success at modest targets ought to be recorded, since this could give a valuable basis for employment. It is hard to achieve this, however, within a system set up to deal uniformly with all students. Equity for different ethnic groups and gender equity are also issues which bridge the curriculum-assessment interface. It is well established that differences of question style and test context can produce variations of overall performance between boys and girls and across different cultural backgrounds. Such bias has to be tackled in the classroom as well as in setting questions, to avoid preferential appeal to one group rather than another.

A particularly difficult problem is presented by students who have to be taught and examined in their second language, *i.e.* one which differs from the language spoken in their homes. To an extent – and where appropriate – this can be alleviated by using assessment methods which do not depend heavily on fluency in the language. Some authorities see the need to devote special resources to minorities, to overcome the obstacles which prevent them from taking full advantage of educational opportunities. Bias in tests is a matter for legal challenge in some countries, and hence has caused closer attention to the defensibility of assessment practices in this regard. A basic problem is thus to arrive at assessment systems which are equitable across the diversity of students but are nevertheless valid in relation to common outcome criteria.

For students to leave school with a record which only shows failure should be unacceptable, but to pretend that all have succeeded is to devalue the record of achievement for all. Some argue that the harsh outcomes of recorded failure have to be accepted, partly because students themselves should be held accountable and partly because leniency merely secures a dubious short-term advantage at the expense of pressures for future improvement. Perhaps the most hopeful approach is to record all performance against a scale of criteria which are exemplars of progression. Then students do not fail – all that is at issue is the level at which they can succeed. Some states in *Australia* give extra resources to schools with poor results. In the *United States*, both withdrawal of resources and provision of extra resources for poorly performing schools have been tried. In the State of Kentucky, high performance is rewarded and poor performance can also lead to extra resources, but only with external monitoring of the school's improvement policy

Reporting and accountability

The form in which tests and examinations are reported depends on the purposes and intended audience. Most valuable in formative terms is the closely contextualised assessment addressed by the teacher to the student alone. At the other end of the spectrum lie those reports on tests of samples of students, designed, for example, to illuminate students' understanding of key mathematical concepts at particular ages. Here the audience is not the students taking the test, nor even their teachers, but those experts concerned with curriculum and assessment construction and evaluation. Good examples are the *Japanese* and *New Zealand* national tests on samples of students, carried out at five-year intervals in different subjects. The results of formative assessments can also be used for reporting on groups of students. Selected and aggregated sets of such results can inform planning at school and at regional or national levels, though such practice would be more evident if a culture of evaluation for improvement of teaching were better established.

National tests are sometimes given to whole populations, in which case the audience for the summary reports is widened to include students and parents, teachers and schools. This is the case with the *British* and *French* national tests of core subjects at key stages. Ostensibly, at least in *France*, the reason for whole population (or census) testing as opposed to sampling is pedagogical. It enables students, parents and teachers to see the individual's performance (which is not published) against national criteria and norms, and to identify areas for improvement. When tests attain this dimension, however, they attract national attention and the results are reported in the media. They take on, sometimes deliberately as in the *British* case, the function of system accountability at national level and school accountability at the local community level; averages of student-performance data become indicators for parents choosing schools. Furthermore, carefully standardised test items permit longitudinal comparison of the progress of particular cohorts of students in different secondary schools over periods of time. This enables fairer comparison of schools than the reporting of raw data of student performance, which to a considerable extent merely reflects the nature of their student intake.

A school can only be held accountable for performance outcomes in relation to its student intake and the resources and other forms of support given to it. Some systems try to allow for quality of student entry and other contextual features outside a school's control, which might affect its performance. For this to happen, performance data have to be complemented by a wide range of other information. The use of student performance data adjusted for other factors to give an "added value" element to schools' performance on national tests has been explored in *France* and *Britain* and in some states in the *United States*. Both interpretation and publication of such data may be difficult – even contentious – for strong action aimed at changing the schools methods or management may follow. If the school is deemed "weak" or "failing" it may even be closed down.

The *New Zealand* Minister of Education asked his ministry to look at ways of centrally collating teacher-collected schoolwide information, to assist with outcome-trend analysis and population sub-group analysis. A number of challenges was posed in meeting this request, by the degree of interpretation afforded by the relatively broad curriculum objectives, and the lack of validity and reliability checks on the assessment tools which teachers use. Hence this school-based information cannot be used for external accountability or school comparison purposes, notwithstanding a common recording and reporting format. *Canada* has undertaken development work on an indicator resource or database. Six indicator areas were chosen for initial development, all important goals for *Canadian* education systems: accessibility, student flows, school/work transitions, achievement, citizenship and satisfaction. They are not mutually exclusive, but interconnected parts of a whole that together provide a comprehensive, coherent picture of student and system performance.

Reporting a school's achievements can be made fairer by adding other evidence to the student performance data, embedding these data in a range of indicators of school performance such as student attendance or students' extra-curricular activities. There are as yet few examples of this being attempted in the public sector, but private schools in most countries have considerable experience of "selling" themselves in this way. National inspectorates can mediate student performance data in their own reporting on the quality of education in the schools they visit. They also offer a means of identifying aspects for improvement within a school, including its assessment system. Inspection procedures – to determine that a full set of curriculum opportunities is being provided – and measures of intake performance and of socio-economic background, might be seen as essential complements to data on performance of students, in arriving at fair judgements of a school and in proposing action to promote improvement.

Thus in *New Zealand*, the Education Review Office has the role of auditing schools' practices in relation to management, pedagogy and evaluation. Strong reliance on inspection by external teams is a feature of policy both in *Belgium* and in the *United Kingdom* (see OECD/CERI, 1995*a* and 1995*b*). However, just as many critics maintain that national testing, even if conducted largely by teachers themselves, cannot properly measure the quality of teaching and learning across the whole spectrum of schools' activities, some are equally sceptical about external inspectors arriving at a true judgement on the basis of a few days' visit. These critics of an external, standards-driven model of assessment would prefer self-appraisal by teachers and schools. Self-appraisal can of course be combined with the use of external indicators such as student performance data and might be made the basis for agreed reporting procedures for visits by peer groups and inspectors as in New York State.

Whilst the certification purpose, and the formative purpose for individual students, require a result to be provided for every student, the other purposes can be met by testing only samples of the population (except perhaps in the case of very small schools, or in the case of minorities for whom the sample may have to be enhanced to give a reliable result). For example, *Canada*, *Flemish Belgium*, *New Zealand* and the *United States* all use national sampling surveys which, in accordance with their formative purpose are necessarily criterion-referenced. Apart from reducing total cost, the use of sampling has the advantage that different tests can be given to different sub-samples so that a wider range of outcomes (*i.e.* wider than blanket testing can cover within the same time period) can be explored. Sampling can also permit the use of richer text formats, requiring, for example, the analysis of open-ended questions, and extended responses. If a full cohort is tested, as has been the case for some years in primary schools in some Australian states, and in several state-accountability systems in the United States, machine-scorable responses are needed if costs are to be contained.

The focus of reporting in most countries is increasingly the performance of schools, groups of schools (districts or states) or the system as a whole, with aggregated student-performance data as the key outcomes measure. This has long been the case – at least for system-level performance – in the United States, where this approach was bolstered in the 1960s and 1970s by the publication of international studies by the IEA, purporting to show the comparative performance of American students in core subjects against students in a range of other countries. One example is the change of National Association for Educational Progress (NAEP) tests from sampling in such a way that reporting could only be at national level, to designing studies so that results can be reported and compared at individual state level. As the countries participating in IEA studies have different educational goals and values, curricula, school organisations, and even epistemological understandings of what constitutes the subjects in which student performances are being compared, critics are sceptical about the validity of these comparisons. However, in the United States, and to a lesser extent in Great Britain, New Zealand, Canada and Australia, reports of these international tests were influential in the educational debate about standards.

Sampling surveys have been influential. National surveys, notably across constituent states in a federal system, have revealed significant trends and variations in performance outcomes – the NAEP studies in the United States are an example. They also serve to help teachers see how their students' achievements compare with those of others. Similarly, international surveys have been regarded in many countries as a judgement of the success of their systems. An important limitation with all such data – often overlooked – is that students' opportunities to acquire any particular knowledge or skill are as important in determining test outcomes as the quality of their learning efforts and the teaching they receive. It can be demonstrated that the degrees of mismatch between national or international tests and the curricula followed in individual schools can explain a large proportion of the variations which are – incorrectly – regarded as indices of teaching quality.

In most countries this focus on aggregated student-performance data is relatively recent if it exists at all. Indeed, many European countries (Germany, Denmark, Ireland, Italy, Spain) focus still on individual students' performance, for which neither schools nor the system are held to account. A law in Denmark forbids the publication of individual students' results and the reporting of comparative performances across schools or regions; nationally-produced performance indicators or league tables are not to be used. The government publishes advice to schools on how they should inform the public about the results of their work. In *Germany*, there is no access to aggregated data on student performance which could be used to report comparatively on the performance of schools.

In *Japan*, there is fierce competition to enter the better upper-secondary schools, which has given rise to an unofficial "league table" of schools. A recent *Japanese* Government report is sharply critical of the effects of this competition, both on the implemented curriculum of the lower secondary schools and on students who, solely on the basis of standardised test results, are often led to take courses for which they have little interest or aptitude. There is something of a paradox here: some analyses of IEA data suggest that *Japanese* students perform very well comparatively in mathematics and science and that the school effect is relatively small in that country. In general however, those countries with high quality education, where teachers have relatively high status, are those where reporting of performance standards is least widespread. These countries are understandably reluctant to jeopardise this quality by importing accountability models from apparently less successful systems.

The most traditional forms of assessment, secondary leaving certificates and university entrance examinations, were rarely aggregated or reported on until recently. Students received their grades and chief examiners usually reported back to schools and teachers on the national overall performance of students, subject-by-subject. This remains the pattern of reporting in *Ireland* and *Australia*, whereas in *England and Wales* schools are now obliged to publish their aggregated results. The practice of the International Baccalaureate is similar to the older British system. In *Germany*, the *abitur* is set and marked by the teachers themselves, but there is monitoring by state officials. No "reporting" in the wider sense occurs. However, there are in the KMK, the co-ordinating body for the state education ministries, mechanisms for monitoring the performance of students across *Länder*. Where necessary – for example entry to medical schools – the grades awarded in different *Länder* are adjusted up or down to compensate for over-generous teacher assessment in some. The reporting to the central body is done by *land* inspectors and officials.

However, as these formerly elite academic courses become opened up to the majority of students, the examinations are undergoing increased scrutiny. The performance of students at the *baccalauréat* is aggregated at school and regional levels and analysed in the *French* media. Unofficial "league tables" are produced which, over time, can only increase competition for places in the better *lycées* (upper secondary schools). Competition among individual students (and their families) for a restricted number of places in elite higher education institutions is a well documented feature in most OECD countries. Some upper secondary schools are considered better placed than others to help students succeed in the entrance examinations to these universities. Here competition between students is the driving factor. In this interpretation, reporting merely serves its usual function of broadcasting the criteria on the basis of which competition occurs, and may in fact serve the interests of equity in opening up arcane procedures to public scrutiny. However, as the *Japanese* example shows, competition at this level may have a distorting effect on the curriculum lower down the system.

POLICY ISSUES

Assessment, testing and learning

Testing is seen by teachers in many countries as a regrettable necessity which damages good learning and inhibits their work. In part this may be inevitable, but it raises two questions. Can such testing be reformed to reflect teachers' learning aims in more authentic and acceptable ways? Is a better match possible between teachers' formative work, their summative responsibilities, and the use of external methods? Some differences here might lie in assumptions made by the different agencies involved about the inter-relationship between testing and good teaching and learning. For example, an administrator might regard a multiple choice test as an economical and quick method of testing a wide range of syllabus content which avoids many problems of bias and of reliable marking. Whilst teachers and learning experts might agree that the tests have these features, they would also be keenly aware that teachers can drill students to do well in such tests. Moreover, the pressure to do so leads to an atomised approach to learning and inhibits the devotion of time to activities which are known to enhance deeper understanding, notably discussion and reflection on students' own more extended efforts to express their learning.

Several countries have seen this tension as a policy issue. In *Finland* – where a reform programme includes a new aim of encouraging students to select and pursue their own targets to enhance their responsibility and maturity as learners – there is concern about the tension between such a pattern of work and the pressures of any new national examination. *Norway* judges that external tests would exert pressure on schools to set students according to ability. For this reason such tests are ruled out, because they would thereby be in conflict with the schools' responsibility to promote social integration. *Flemish Belgium* abandoned the external component of the end of secondary school examination in 1991 – it was not seen to be serving any useful purpose and it was thought to be more important to trust schools entirely, whilst using sample surveys to monitor the system as a whole. In the State of Queensland, external school-leaving examinations were abandoned in 1982. Since then schools have collaborated in regional groups, to build up over many years, and within the state's framework, a system of peer review and audit of their curriculum plans and assessment results. In *Germany*, there is some tension between those *Länder* which use external assessment of the *abitur*, Bavaria, for example, and those which rely entirely on teacher assessment. The issue becomes more acute when high-stakes outcomes, such as entry to medical schools, are decided by national committees, which "weight" the various *abiturs*.

Assessment and the curriculum

Assessment often has the effect of distorting the curriculum. There is an inevitable tendency to devalue any learning aims which are difficult to assess by the means currently acceptable; examples are practical work, open-ended projects which cannot be attempted in the short time possible for formal tests, and measures of motivation and of students' values. This distorting effect might take effect when curricula are being formulated, or at the implementation stage if assessment cannot reflect aspects of the formulation. More generally, trends in assessment practices interact with trends in curriculum change. As innovations develop, it is normal to evaluate the ways in which students respond: it is important also to explore how assumptions or actions about assessment practice are shaping the development, or are being shaped by its impact.

Students and assessment

A further interaction is the effect that assessment and testing has on students' learning work and on their perceptions of schooling. In some countries, notably *Norway* and *Finland*, emphasis is being given to developing students' self-assessment. The belief is that learning will improve if students take more responsibility for themselves and if they develop a better overview of the structures and purposes of their learning. Self-assessment is a necessary skill if lifelong learning is to be made effective; in most post-school learning the adult does not have access to frequent independent assessment.

Reforms in assessment place heavy burdens. Any policy should aim to share these burdens with others so that they do not fall entirely on teachers. This is one amongst several reasons why the role that students might play in their own assessment is emerging as a new and important issue. It seems that students – at least at secondary school level – are capable of assessing their own progress in ways that help them to take more responsibility for their own learning. In addition, self-assessment helps make it possible for the teacher to cope with the daunting task of keeping track of the wide ranging and changing needs of a classroom full of students.

As with the case of teachers' formative assessments, however, it is not easy for students to grow into this new role. They have to be guided, first to come to understand the aims of their learning and the criteria for judging success. There is evidence that most students lack such understanding and move through learning routines without grasping their structure or their purpose. If they acquire the understanding, then they have to learn to be realistic, and come to see that they disadvantage themselves if they make judgements that are either too optimistic or too pessimistic. Developments in these directions will make assessment practices fully consonant with, and capable of enriching, the main thrust of improvements in learning methods which have derived from constructivist models. Such models stress that, to be effective, learning has to be meaningful and so has to be based on and develop from the individual's own set of understandings – not superimposed on these as a meaningless and disconnected overlay.

Students are in general driven by the "cash-value" of external certificate tests; their beliefs about the learning habits needed to secure good results are powerful drives for their work. Various alternatives to terminal examinations – using module-by-module assessments and graded assessment by which students build up a portfolio of attested achievements – have been traditional in some systems and are innovations in others. The students' perspectives and beliefs within such different systems ought to be explored more thoroughly. One recent trend is to require summative data for students to be detailed, in the form of a profile of achievements or a portfolio of work. This provides richer data on which selectors can make sensitive judgements, and can perhaps also be a guide for those teaching a student in the next stage of education (so serving partly as formative). Several states in the United States, notably Vermont, have developed this approach, and the British development of "Records of Achievement" used a similar approach. Such portfolios can involve negotiation with students, helping them become more responsible for and aware of their own progress in learning, and enhancing their self-confidence. Likewise, increasingly sophisticated approaches to accountability seek to interpret a profile of outcomes, thereby to inform corrective action and perhaps to use formatively for a system as a whole.

Teachers' roles in assessment

Different systems embody very different beliefs about the role of teachers in assessment. One view is that teachers' work is essentially formative, and that this requires such a different approach from the summative that the two cannot be related. From this perspective only externally-set tests are reliable enough, and command the confidence that are essential for summative testing. The teacher has to improve the formative work – often seen as not problematic – and respond to the pressures that the work of the external testers create. A different scenario arises if teachers are to take part in the summative assessment of their own students, perhaps with a tension between the two roles of supporting their students and evaluating them. Some argue that it is essential to separate evidence for each purpose, others that much of what might be collected and recorded might serve both purposes, albeit with different interpretations and aggregations between the two.

The evidence is that in at least some countries teachers are not well-equipped in assessment skills, making surprisingly few formative assessments and relying mainly on end-of-topic or end-of-term tests, which are of varying quality and which cannot have a formative effect. This might be one reason why the extent of the ranges in students' understanding in many subject areas has been revealed in research but has not been seen as a serious problem by many teachers. It seems to follow, however, that it will not be possible to act on the information that effective formative assessment would reveal without quite radical changes in pedagogy. For this reason formative assessment cannot just be added on to existing practice as a useful extra, but will require investment of resources and the involvement of teachers. The development must include not only the means to collect and interpret assessment information, but also the changes in pedagogy required, if teaching is to respond more effectively to the wide range of student needs in any one classroom.

To supplement their own resources, teachers may be required to use external tests or items and must then understand the strategies that lie behind their construction. Teachers' methods and procedures are trusted to provide certification in some countries and not in others. This raises questions about teachers having the necessary skills, about the reliability and validity of their judgements, and about bias in their approach, given that their first commitment is to students and parents rather than to national standards or accountability. There can be tensions between the different functions of assessment, since items and procedures designed for one purpose may not be appropriate for another. Furthermore, the problem of securing synergy between different functions – notably between the formative and summative assessment roles which might be required of teachers – may be a delicate one. For example, answers to a single question or to a single multiple-choice item may be enough to help choose the next step in a classroom, where subsequent discussion can expose and correct any possible misinterpretation of the evidence. In an external test, however, such exchange and correction is not possible and other ways to guide against misinterpretation must be used. Several countries combine external test data with teachers' own data and judgements of their students for certification and accountability purposes.

Teachers who are to become more effective in the use of assessment will need a firm base of subject knowledge and a range of teaching options. They will need assessment expertise and help in terms of matching assessment to the curriculum structures they are trying to develop. It may be particularly difficult to improve current practice in formative assessment – which is weak – given that this may require a change in working habits built up over many years. Teachers will also have a summative role, and find the optimum mix between external agencies and pressures and their own areas of responsibility hard to achieve. It is essential for there to be understanding and mutual respect in the partnerships that should be evolved. For teachers, the need is to reflect on the place of assessment in their pedagogy, to internalise and come to terms with changes in their roles and in their practice. Extensive preparation, training and support materials – and in particular new means to share assessment practices and standards with peers – seem to be essential if real improvement is to be secured.

Diversity, differentiation and progression

If pedagogy is to provide for the wide range of learning needs and progress amongst students, then this has implications for the structure of any curriculum, whether it be a national framework or one teacher's own planning guide. A curriculum cannot be expressed as a set of topics tied to the successive years of schooling. It has to have a structure which is not strongly linked to age, but which expresses the sequence of learning achievements through which students make progress. Such a framework will set out targets for students in relation to the levels already reached, thereby offering the possibility of success, whether the student is in the top percentile, the bottom one, or anywhere between. The task of formative assessment is then clear. The formulation of such sequences, within every particular subject and in different cultures, can only be done through a marriage between assumptions concerning the epistemology and educational contribution of the subject, the pedagogy and the nature of students' learning. The task is a formidable one that will require full use of present insights to achieve first formulations and new empirical work to refine those efforts. Several countries are attempting such formulations, which are recognised to be ambitious. *New Zealand*, for example, formulates each main aspect of every new curriculum in terms of an 8-level scheme of criteria, for progression across the whole range of expectations in compulsory schooling.

Criterion-referenced assessment is essential to the approach outlined here. A norm-referenced approach sorts students by distinguishing the proportions of common tasks which different students are able to tackle. This has the particular disadvantage that those with lowest achievement may fail to do anything worthwhile with the majority of the tasks. If standards are to mean that every child must have an opportunity to learn everything specified, then this may lead to attempts to teach material to some for whom it will be unintelligible. A criterion-referenced approach can present a graded set of tasks so that those of low achievement are distinguished by the level of the tasks with which they are able to succeed. A choice between these two approaches is not merely a choice between assessment techniques, but requires consistently-related choices of classroom teaching methods and school policies on differentiation.

Given such a scenario, summative assessments also have to be structured to match the curriculum and the pedagogy. The assessment for each student should be tuned to the levels of achievement at which that student can largely succeed while showing limitations in going further. This means that the summative system will have to be highly differentiated, and that students may be distinguished, not by marks ranging from 10 per cent to 90 per cent, for instance, but by those levels at which they can achieve (say) 80 per cent. Unless something like this can be done, we might go on sending out of school students carrying only a badge of failure and no proof of any competence or capability.

External tests

Several of the above arguments indicate the need for supportive consistency between summative assessment practices and pressures and the needs of formative assessment. It must not be assumed however that formative assessment should be entrusted entirely to the internal work of schools. External stimulus and support are essential. Externally-provided instruments and guides to procedures can help in ensuring equity in assessment. They can help schools to work with a common understanding of national or regional standards, thereby strengthening a criterion-referenced basis against the natural tendency to work within class or school norms. In *Scotland*, the government provides national banks of items with guidelines for their use, but it is up to teachers to decide when best to use them. The optimum combination between external and school-based assessments, in determining summative results of great importance to individual students and to their schools, is hard to find. As has been pointed out, it may be as much determined by traditions and by the public esteem of teachers and schools as by technical factors.

External summative assessments can achieve adequate validity in relation to some learning aims if they can take substantial time and can deploy a range of methods. Examples are the new methods being explored for so-called "performance assessments" in the *United States*, and the wide range of methods used in some public examinations and in performance surveys in the *United Kingdom*. All, however, underline that such methods can be expensive, and so raise the question of whether the resource might be better used, for instance in improving the quality and calibration of teachers' own assessments. It can be helpful if teachers are involved in setting and marking such examinations, as happens in *Canada* and in the *United Kingdom*. The matriculation exams in *Finland* can be taken on three occasions and are available twice each year, enabling students to space out the work of preparation and cope with the stresses of testing.

Where students are leaving school, or are in transition between different stages of a school system, the need for good quality assessment is clear and external methods might be particularly important in ensuring comparability of standards between different schools. In *New Zealand* tests are given when students first enter school, whilst for other transition points there are external banks of tests on which teachers can draw to check and to calibrate their judgements. The *French* initiative, with diagnostic tests at the start of the school year is a further example. In *Germany*, the transfer to the intermediate school and grammar school often places great strain on students attending the final class at primary schools. Empirical studies on the reliability and accuracy of the decisions on the streams of students selected for transfer reveal that this issue has not yet been satisfactorily resolved. Average marks and the results of test papers reflect merely a fraction of the skills required to achieve success at secondary schools.

The school as a unit

It is increasingly recognised that the school is a key unit in any change or improvement. Such issues as opportunity to learn, uses of inspection and of peer exchange, support for external training, depend as much on school management policies as on individual teachers' actions. There are potential tensions between support of schools and judgement of them. Some national policies require publication of schools' testing and assessment results, seen as a spur to improvement and as needed to inform parental choice. Other systems, which regard such publication as unhelpful or politically unacceptable, emphasise self-evaluation and development by schools. The CERI publication *Schools under Scrutiny* (OECD/CERI, 1995*b*) investigates how the performance of schools is evaluated in seven different OECD countries. The broad set of indicators needed to interpret school performance and the possible use of sampling rather than blanket testing are relevant issues here.

System accountability

Whilst individual teachers and schools may be held accountable for students' learning, this accountability cannot extend to the circumstances over which they have control. Thus, if a survey analysis were to show that performance overall falls as class sizes rise beyond a certain limit, then it may be that central funding policy should be held accountable, rather than individual schools or the system as a whole. A similar argument applies to the case of teacher training, both initial and in-service. It is always arguable that teachers are responsible because they could have worked more skilfully or more conscientiously, that the central authorities are responsible because of inadequate or misinformed support, or that training institutions are at fault because of weaknesses in their programmes. What must be clear, however, is that data on students' performances cannot alone resolve such debates. Careful collection of a broad set of complementary data is essential, both of measurable indicators that can be used in statistical analysis, and of qualitative case studies to illuminate the mechanisms and issues in a different way. Above all is needed a sense of the complexity of the issues and a desire to distil authentic insights, neither of which may fit well in the context of political debate.

REFLECTIONS AND POINTS FOR FURTHER CONSIDERATION

Reforms driven by public or political reaction to perceived shortcomings, even to perceived crises, are hard to manage well. There is risk of counter-reaction from those blamed for the crisis, and if they are driven too fast this can lead to policy vacillations which are very wasteful, or even to breakdown. A clear obstacle to pursuing some desirable paths to change is that the assumptions on which they are based are not understood, let alone accepted, by politicians and the general public. Thus, in some cultures where teachers' own assessments are not trusted, there is no will to invest in improving their reliability or in working to calibrate standards between schools. In most cultures, an unquestioning faith is placed in external tests, causing technical objections to them by professionals to be seen as defensive evasion. Most serious of all, the invalidity of a large proportion of assessment and testing results is not understood.

What is needed is a careful trajectory of change, wherein small steps can be evaluated to check and correct errors, and where the many interest groups can be recruited to make the reforms work. Those seeking fundamental assessment change are up against a particularly difficult obstacle, however, since traditional testing is something that many have experienced and accept without question. The gap in understanding between schools and the many official and other agencies which surround them is also a matter of concern in many countries. It is clear that educators have to devote significant efforts to raising the level of public comprehension of testing and assessment.

A major technical challenge to assessment studies is to find ways of resolving the problems of reliability and generalisability in the area of "performance" or "authentic" assessments. This is particularly so where the assessments are embedded in everyday classroom work, with the intention of using them for formative and summative purposes. Progress here might help in the difficult task of convincing politicians and parents of the importance of formative as opposed to summative assessments. Politicians tend to back away from government involvement in formative work, partly from lack of understanding, partly from a belief that they should raise standards by reliance on external pressures, while avoiding "interference" in the classroom. This separation of formative and summative assessment policies is to the detriment of both. Teachers need more skill and confidence in formative and summative assessment, and in acting on assessment information to meet the diverse needs of students. School and teacher autonomy in providing curriculum diversity requires a matching enhancement of skills and responsibilities in assessment, lest external assessments deny flexibility. Tests to raise standards would be more effective if directed to the processes of learning, the formative rather than the summative stage, as in the *French* initiative described above. Such responsibilities for assessment should form an integral part of teacher professionalism.

In conclusion, it appears that classroom realities in schools are very similar across different countries, whereas the political and public rhetoric about education and assessment can differ widely. Effective dialogue between education professionals and the public is both necessary and difficult to achieve.

For further consideration

Can a central authority say to schools "here are the outcomes and the means by which they will be tested, the rest is up to you"? Not whilst the related determinants, such as resource allocation and teacher training are controlled by that authority. The interplay between developing practice and standard-setting-plus-assessment ought to be creative and exploratory rather than disconnected and prescriptive. Not least this is because society and its needs are changing more rapidly than schools can change, and equitable treatment for all demands constant care to avoid bias in curriculum, pedagogy and assessment. The means will vary in order to achieve a fair reflection of the achievements of diverse groups, but common aims and standards are an entitlement and are desired by all.

Can an assessment system respond to and support any curriculum change, so that curriculum can first be decided with assessment following? No, because assessment and curriculum change must evolve interactively, with assessment suggesting curricular modifications and identifying new aims. Many educational writers assume that assessment-led reform is sure to be unhelpful. There may be a confusion here – for clearly a first priority in any innovation is to formulate its educational aims, but assessment and testing can be powerful tools in securing their realisation. This is not only, or even mainly by exerting pressure on reluctant schools and teachers, but rather by expressing the intentions in concrete operational terms so that their implications for pedagogy and learning can be understood. Reform can be initiated by new assessments or tests, by new programmes for teacher activity supported by in-service training, or by new curriculum formulations, but whichever leads the implications for all have to be followed through.

So, finally, how fast can change be made? Not very, because the system is complex and multi-faceted, requiring innovations to be comprehensively planned and introduced with care if unintended consequences are to be avoided. Such consequences can damage a reform and may even make a good idea seem inappropriate. Part of the complex of processes is the public's understanding and acceptance of the change, part the readiness of teachers to implement it. There is a delicate balance to be struck. On the one hand is the professional autonomy of teachers and of institutions. On the other is the public interest in supporting social change, in defining the preparation of future citizens and in ensuring accountability for expenditure. The impetus for reform can arise from either, but all concerned must be fully persuaded.

TEACHERS AND THEIR PROFESSIONAL DEVELOPMENT

INTRODUCTION

It is argued here that policies for the professional development of teachers should be seen in the wider context of systemic reform. The basic insight of systemic reform is to suggest that any one element of an education system (such as teacher development) cannot be considered in isolation from other elements. Hence, in this chapter, teacher development is regarded as closely related to the other matters dealt with in this report, curriculum and assessment in particular. This need not be an instrumental relationship, such as providing specific teacher training for implementation of a new syllabus or assessment regime. Rather it is a dynamic interaction, as for instance when curriculum innovation emerges from sustained co-operation among teachers.

Teachers need to be involved throughout the education reform process if it is to have a serious chance of success. The pace of change in education and its environment is fast, while the turnover of personnel is low. New policies must thus be implemented largely by the existing corps of teachers. Hence, in terms of priorities, it is more urgent to support in-service development than to change the selection or training of new teachers, crucial though these latter are over the longer term. Moreover, policies for the initial training of teachers are increasingly focused on the school, which makes appropriate the priority given here to professional development. Teachers are seen as part of a team, with collective responsibilities for developing curriculum and assessment practice in dialogue with the local community. Professional development seen in this light is not something separate or momentary, but part of an organic process of change and adaptation.

POLICY ISSUES IN PROFESSIONAL DEVELOPMENT

Some decades ago, the job structure was stable and the demands on employees varied little. Few positions in politics, business or social life called for dynamic qualities such as independent thinking, initiative, ability to co-operate or to seek responsibility. School was expected to prepare young people to be diligent and disciplined, ready to perform the tasks other people had set. To this end pre-defined knowledge, competences, and values were stored in curricula, tests and accredited textbooks. The main characteristics of this culture, to which teaching and learning are still largely attuned, are as follows (Posch, 1994):

- A *predominance of systematic knowledge*. High priority is given to established facts derived in particular from universities, low priority to personal experience and controversial areas of knowledge.

- *Specialisation*. Knowledge is compartmentalised, largely in accordance with academic disciplines, to give teaching and learning a clear and predictable structure. Complex, real-life situations tend to be disregarded because they cross these boundaries.

- A *transmission mode of teaching*. The student is encouraged to grasp the system-atic character of knowledge, but discouraged from generating knowledge and handling it reflectively.

- A *prevalence of top-down communication*. This facilitates curricular and classroom control, but discourages co-operation among students and teachers, self-control, networking across school boundaries, and initiative-taking.

For the last two decades, the limitations of this approach have attracted much criticism from different sources. One example of this arises as the importance of so-called key qualifications is increasingly recognised: the ability to co-operate and work in teams, to communicate in one's mother tongue and in at least one other lan-guage, to identify and solve problems, to be media-literate and to have mastered the techniques for lifelong learning. These abilities appear more and more to be the threshold conditions for participation in work and in society, but, it is con-tended, schools fail to promote their achievement. Another reason for criticism also has to do with changes in the world of work, but with a quite different perspective. It notes that an increasing number of students find it difficult to connect their school experience with a positive future vision for themselves, and therefore lose any motivation to succeed at school. Academic success, defined in terms of mastery of the contents of traditional school subjects, is no longer a guarantee of success in the labour market. Increasing numbers of citizens are unlikely to have careers in the future, but will have to sell their skills on a temporary-contract basis. In addition, they will have continuously to retrain, as skills become obsolescent. From different starting points, both these illustrations point to the same question: how can schools become more effective at fostering the development of students as autonomous, self-regulating, and self-evaluating learners, enabled to construct their own futures? Attempts to respond to this question demand a new articulation of the aims and processes of education and require changes at all levels of the system. They affect the curriculum, the organisation of teaching, learning and assessment, and the interaction of individual teachers with individual students.

The culture of teaching and learning in the future will have to come to terms with conflicting demands. It will have to retain the strengths of static elements stressing the transmission of predefined content, while complementing this with dynamic qualities, with their emphasis on knowledge-access routes and process-learning contexts. The main challenge for education will be to shape this shift of emphasis constructively, away from heavy reliance on the static conception of the past to a more dynamic interpretation of teaching and learning. Teachers play a crucial role in this change process and professional development is on the top of policy agenda in many countries. Thus the Irish report entitled *Charting our Education Future* (Ireland, 1995, p. 125) states that "the capacity of the education system to cope with and lead change is critically dependent on developing the necessary attitudinal and professional competences of the teaching profession".

Some key questions

- A profession that has to cope with increasingly complex situations cannot be told what to do, but has to develop an intrinsic interest in continuous development. How can this interest be stimulated?

- Professional development is not only an individual matter, but more and more a co-operative endeavour involving partners inside and outside the profession. How can the development of these networks be supported?

- Equity is a pressing concern in many countries, not only for considerations of social justice but also for the pragmatic considerations of social and economic stability, even survival. As a result, teachers have to deal with increasing heterogeneity of the student population. What changes in working structures and opportunities for professional development have to be created, to meet this enormous challenge?

- Tasks have increasingly to be delegated to teachers and schools, because beyond a certain complexity and variety, problems cannot be solved *for* the practitioners, but rather, *by them*, taking account of the local situation. Which tasks have to remain a national concern in order to safeguard common public interests?

- Increasing autonomy is associated necessarily with calls for accountability. By what means can accountability be secured without crippling local initiatives?

- Policy initiatives in whatever area interact critically with professional development, itself a vital concern. Examples are found in *curriculum* – for instance the creation of space for local decision-making with respect to educational aims; *organisation* – as with finding time for planning and reflection; and *assessment* – issues such as local responsibility for grading. How can a systemic approach be realised which, on the one hand concentrates on basic require-ments (to keep costs under control), and on the other achieves maximum effectiveness?

THE CHANGING ROLE OF TEACHERS

A starting point for addressing these questions is to ask what are the new chal-lenges confronting teachers, that define new agendas for professional development. Some of these challenges and their implications will now be discussed.

Changing expectations of students

The student is a contributor to the educational process, insofar as the aims of education are not achievable directly, but only by stimulating and directing activi-ties of the learner. Whilst this has always been so, it has added importance with the enormous expansion of knowledge. Students may invest energy in educational tasks or evade them, but are increasingly likely to limit themselves to learning which appears meaningful to them and which they can influence, in other words which they see as legitimate in their own terms. This individuality has to do with the weakening of established social networks and patterns of behaviour, with the wider range of options outside school, and with the contradictory signals by which they are confronted from early life, such as short-term versus deferred gratification.

Probably one of the most important factors is the dramatically changing author-ity relationship in families. The interaction between parents and children is becom-ing more like a partnership in which arguments are replacing orders and commands. What is allowed and not allowed has become a matter of negotiation between par-ents and children, with the age at which this process starts still decreasing, so that more and more children meet school against a background of such experience. At school, however, they meet a context in which they have hardly any influence on procedures. Problems in the interaction between teachers and students can often be explained by this clash of a "negotiation culture" with a "command culture", because the teacher's traditional position as authority figure no longer corresponds with the way parents relate to their children.

Teachers through their formal authority are much less able than in the past to mandate learning activities and to control the educational process. They have to be able to negotiate with their students to legitimate learning activities, since external legitimisation is unlikely to offer sufficient credibility. This dramatic role change is illustrated in *Denmark*: "At each form-level and in each subject, the teacher and the student shall co-operate continuously on determining the objectives (...). The establishment of working methods and the selection of subject matter shall as far as possible take place in co-operation between teachers and students" (Denmark, 1994, p. 10).

The quest for dynamic qualities

The growing complexity of public and private economic developments appears to be one of the major factors behind decentralisation of decision-making structures. A significant aspect is the decrease of problem-solving capacity within the large socio-economic systems and centralised power-structures of society. This is illustrated in tendencies to "privatise" public services, and to devolve to individual citizens responsibility for environmental quality, for social security and even for safety. Citizens will have to cope with low-structured situations, be able to define problems, take positions and accept responsibility for them.

This objective need for dynamic qualities is matched by an increasing subjective quest among the young to be taken seriously, to be empowered to influence their conditions of life and affect their environment. There seems to be a considerable incongruity between the diversity of pressures to which young people are subject and their own opportunity to exert influence. A quotation from a skinhead in a radio report gives a vivid illustration: "I throw stones, therefore I am". Vandalism is a way of leaving personal traces in one's environment. There appears to be a growing need for frameworks in which the young can contribute to shaping their environment in a responsible and constructive way, thereby experiencing that they matter in society. Acting on the environment is seen as a way to cope with complexity.

An example of environmental involvement is the *Environment and School Initiatives* (ENSI) project (see, for example: OECD/CERI, 1991; Elliott, 1994; Posch, 1994). This project was designed as a piece of cross-national curriculum development in which schools introduced environmental education curricula that were consistent with two basic aims. One of these was to help students develop an understanding of the complex relationships between human beings and their environment, using interdisciplinary learning and generation of knowledge about their environment. The other was to foster a learning process which requires students to develop dynamic qualities, such as exercising initiative, accepting responsibility and taking action to resolve real environmental problems within their locality. Such examples of curricular developments have considerable implications for the role of the teacher as well as for curriculum and the organisation of work in school. Teachers will have to be actively prepared to create conditions in which learning is not only considered to be useful for the future, but valid for the present.

Changes in the access routes to knowledge and experience

School is an element of society and heavily influenced by the values dominant in society. Traditionally, society influenced teachers through syllabuses, textbooks, legal regulations, peer and parental pressures. The teacher was regarded as the main mediator to the learner of social values and their manifestations. This view has to change as the traditional barriers between subjects, classroom activities and the world outside are giving way. Increasingly, the knowledge offered by schools can also be gained outside school, and information technology is likely to play an ever greater role. However, the more complex, variable and unpredictable the environment, the more essential the school becomes as a source of direct educational experience. Partnerships and networks will have to be established to stimulate use by students of a broad spectrum of learning resources. There are implications for the teacher's role:

- teachers lose their monopoly on information and thereby lose an important source of social control. They have to develop a new self-understanding, as facilitators and mediators of their students' interactions with a variety of human and material resources;

- the sources of information and experience external to the school are less systematic, and do not fit the traditional standards of quality associated with reproducing predefined academic structures of knowledge. Teachers, less able to rely on established standards, have to define quality criteria specific to learning situations and in negotiation with students;

- teachers have not only to assist students to make use of knowledge from a variety of sources, but also to check its significance and credibility.

The last point was discussed in the Danish parliament: "Technological development has led to a stream of information which is at the same time easily accessible and almost inexhaustible. It is therefore more important than ever before that students acquire the skills which enable them to be selective in relation to this massive spread of information" (Denmark, 1992b, p. 245). That official policy statement goes farther: "The Folkeskole should provide an antithesis to all this [exposure to a wide range of stimuli from the new media]. Instead of attempting to compete with the media on their own terms, the school should attempt to help the students to see things as a whole, and adopt methods which give children the time to work with things in depth and to become involved in what they are doing" (op. cit.).

Public involvement in education and the building of school-community networks were relatively marginal – even regarded as counterproductive – as long as the teacher's task was limited to the transmission of defined information and skills. They become paramount, however, once the task extends to experiences which embrace more than the individual teacher and school can offer. The necessary collaboration can take many forms, such as "designing 'real world' performance tasks, serving on expert panels to judge performances, projects or portfolios, sponsoring school-to-work, internship or apprenticeship programmes, and mentoring or tutoring students in need of support" (Slattery, 1995, p. 6). If teachers are to be prepared for these tasks, the provision of industrial and commercial work experience may become an indispensable element in their professional development.

It is important for the relationship between school and community to be interactive, so that students, teachers and the community all profit from these links. A *Danish* statement of educational policy recommends that "the individual school, on the basis of local needs and wishes, be given the opportunity to become a cultural centre in co-operation with local clubs and associations and other interested parties" (Denmark, 1992*a*, p. 6). By way of example, Danish schools were subsequently invited to offer adults the opportunity of participating in instruction in the 8th to 10th grades (Denmark, 1994, p. 4).

Shifts towards integrative structures

Although there are some opposing tendencies, there are indications of a long-term trend to reduce segregative structures in the educational system, as indicated by extending comprehensive schooling, integrating handicapped children and children with behavioural difficulties into the mainstream, increasing cultural diversity, and making provisions to reduce school failure. Equity issues and considerations of social justice have implications for the role of teachers, but go far beyond this to touch basic questions of self-understanding within society. How much difference can society accommodate without major social tensions? How much difference does society need for its democratic, economic and cultural development? Neglect of equity concerns can lead to enormous social costs as some become excluded. The curriculum must be designed to offer positive visions of the future to those at risk of such exclusion, so that all will be enabled to participate actively in society. For teachers this means identifying and stimulating the strengths of students – as diverse as they are – and not merely looking for and trying to meet deficits. It means developing constructive ways to cope with status differences among students. It asks teachers to give to students responsibilities which the students recognise to be important, and others which the students can shape, or in Tenbruck's (1975) terms, which have "significance value" and not only "utility value" for them.

Demands for public accountability

In many countries teachers and schools have traditionally been the last link in a chain of local, regional and central administrative regulations. At present we see a tendency in these countries to increase the autonomy of schools. Decentralisation is particularly conspicuous in some of the former communist countries. In an extreme example, the *Czech Republic* moved from a heavily-centralised system to one in which schools can obtain the status of legal entities. In such a case the director appoints staff, determines the contracts, work load and salary, is responsible for evaluation and decides part of the curriculum. Decentralisation is partly the result of a general trend to deregulate public institutions following a market ideology, and partly a result of the increasing complexity of educational demands on schools, which have caused some established top-down hierarchical patterns to become counter-productive. Both developments have promoted changes in the relationship between practitioners and the educational administration. The role of the teacher has been redefined to include certain organisational responsibilities, such as participation in the selection and organisation of educational content and the in-service education of teachers.

Increased autonomy for schools has reduced the ability of authorities to influence the educational process through input factors, such as prescribed curricula, regulation of instructional organisation and time structure, prescribed materials and modes of assessment. As decision-making power is devolved to the school and to the individual teacher, public interest grows to secure influence on the educational processes by other means. This is generally done via the output of the system. In other words, if teachers receive increased discretion with respect to the planning of the educational process, they are held accountable to a much higher degree than if they are just implementing legal or administrative requirements.

These general remarks have to be qualified in a number of ways, however. In order to judge changes in system control one has to take national traditions into account. Devolution of input control to schools means one thing where there is a centralist baseline, as in the *German-speaking* countries. It means another in traditionally deregulated countries such as the *Netherlands*, or those with a strong market ideology such as the Anglo-Saxon countries. Moreover, the question "autonomy for whom?" is answered quite differently depending on the cultural traditions. It might be the teacher, the school leader, the school board, the community or the regional education authority. Differences in these matters can create considerable confusions. In centralised systems the autonomy of the individual teacher can be relatively high, there being little local control and the responsible institution being far away. Likewise, individual teacher-autonomy can be very small in a decentralised system, in which much power is invested in the headteacher or local school board.

There is a great variety of approaches to ensure accountability, the most common being: self-evaluation; peer evaluation; evaluation by inspection; evaluation by standardised tests based on quality indicators. They differ in:

- their closeness to the teaching and learning process, self-evaluation being closer than inspection or standardised tests;
- the roles practitioners play in shaping the evaluation process, practitioners being in full control of self-evaluation but not at all involved in standardised tests;
- their consequences: at one end of the spectrum is trust in the market mechanism, so that evaluation results are published and are expected to influence parental choice and thereby the resources that a school receives; at the

other end is what one might call trust in guidance strategies, where the results of the evaluation are primarily used for feedback dealing with strengths and weaknesses.

Whilst it may seem desirable to collect ever more sophisticated information in order to identify effective or ineffective schools, this cannot be an end in itself, but must lead to effective mechanisms for change where needed. There are countries (*German-speaking*) where there is practically no evaluation at all, but in these countries input control – such as regulations with respect to teacher training, curriculum, and assessment procedures – is still very strong. An important policy issue is to find a balance between state control, professional control and accountability to the community. The balance must reflect not only the extent of school autonomy, but the level of resources and infrastructural support enabling that autonomy to be used constructively. There is otherwise the danger that it is blame which is decentralised while power remains at the centre. Rather than empowering the local level, decentralisation may reduce its ability to influence the conditions of work, making it too dependent on market forces and mobile consumers. It is important for the community to see the school not merely as a reactive institution but as a proactive one, that portrays a vision of society to which teachers and students contribute. This vision must receive due consideration in all decision-making.

In the context of role changes affecting teachers, a strong element of professional self-government appears to be indispensable to any concept of accountability, with the policy implication being that this responsibility should be assigned to schools. Every school should then develop and sustain an effective system of professional self-government, as illustrated in the following model (Elliott, 1983):

- accountability is considered as a professional responsibility and controlled by the profession. A protected space is created in which critical reflection on individual and collective performance and on alternatives is institutionalised without external interference;

- it is considered a professional responsibility to engage in dialogue with students, parents, administrators and community members. This dialogue is considered to be a contribution to school development;

- teachers and schools are encouraged to publish the result of their reflection and innovation process, thus facilitating a critical discussion by their peers and contributing to a professional knowledge base.

This model of accountability is based on a concept of reflective teaching (see, for example, Altrichter *et al.*, 1993) and devolves responsibility for the development of quality to teachers and schools. It appears to be well suited to deal constructively with the increasing pressures for institutional change, since accountability becomes integrated in the broader task of curriculum and school development.

Such role changes for teachers pose considerably higher demands than their traditional task of transmitting predefined sets of information. Teachers lose to an extent the safety net provided by clear, undisputed standards of quality and have to negotiate them with their students. They become role models as they work towards complex educational aims which require the wholehearted engagement of the student. They themselves need the dynamic skills which they attempt to foster in their students. Larger demands are made on the self-confidence and personalities of teachers, on their ability to communicate with students, to set and legitimate limits.

The challenges also have implications for the curriculum. Moves towards a more dynamic culture of learning imply that the question of what should be taught can only partially be answered by regulation and national curricula. To a considerable degree, teachers have to be involved in the reflection on aims at the school and classroom levels. This quite new aspect of the role of teachers also has implications for the structure of the curriculum and for the assessment system. It implies a move from "single-loop" to "double-loop" learning (Argyris and Schön, 1974). Double-loop learning implies that teachers are expected not only to become more effective and efficient in carrying out their tasks, but also to reflect on – and if necessary modify – goals, structures and roles.

PRINCIPLES RELATING TO PROFESSIONAL DEVELOPMENT

Changes in the concept of professionalism

Traditionally, the concept of professionalism follows the paradigm of "technical rationality" (Schön, 1983), which suggests that there are general solutions to practical problems. These solutions can be developed outside practical situations (in academic or administrative centres), and can be transformed into practitioners' actions by high-level training, publications, regulation, etc. The paradigm of technical rationality implies a separation of theory (knowledge production) and practice (knowledge utilisation), and a separation between professional and customer that is called by Argyris and Schön (1974) a "mystery and mastery" relationship. However, this traditional view of professional development has proved inadequate. Its validity depended on the existence of clear and unambiguous aims, on the predictability of practical situations and effective strategies to cope with them.

Increasingly, any social situation must be regarded as unique, involving its own complex dynamics and value conflicts. In an attempt to match this complexity for the conceptualisation of teachers' professional work, the paradigm of "reflective rationality" has been proposed (Posch and Altrichter, 1992). It is based on the assumption that complex practical situations need specific solutions, being characterised by ambiguous and partially contradictory aims, such as the need to define problems before solutions can be found. Furthermore, problem definitions and the strategies necessary to cope with them must be produced *within* practice by the practitioners in co-operation with others concerned. Subsequently, the situational understanding gained by practitioners reflecting on action can be made accessible to other practitioners – rather that transmitted – to be tested and further developed by them.

Being professional involves the ability to generate context-specific local knowledge in order to enhance the quality of services, so the paradigm of reflective rationality has considerable implications for professional development. Complex practical situations are tackled in co-operation with other professionals and by allowing clients to play important roles in performing and evaluating professional tasks. Services are controlled by those who are involved in their planning and real-isation, but reflective evaluation and negotiation between interacting partners are central. Reflective rationality implies a new balance between individual autonomy and collegial and client-oriented co-operation.

For Stenhouse (1975) an "extended professionalism" of the teaching profession implies the following:

"(…) the commitment to systematic questioning of one's own teaching as a basis for development; the commitment and the skills to study one's own teaching; the concern to question and to test theory in practice by the use of those skills. To these may be added as highly desirable, though perhaps not essential, a readiness to allow other teachers to observe one's work – directly or through recordings – and to discuss it with them on an open and honest basis. In short, the outstanding characteristic of the extended professional is a capacity for autonomous professional self-development through systematic self-study, through the study of the work of other teachers and through the testing of ideas by classroom research procedures".

The implications of this analysis for the professional development of teachers corresponds in many ways with the needs summarised by Lortie (1975, p. 221). These needs involve greater adaptability, whereby changing demands can be met in a proactive, self-confident and reflective way. Although they imply a loss in teacher autonomy as responsibilities are shared with colleagues, collaboration in teaching and decision-making offer increased potential for teacher control. More-over, by sharing knowledge and expertise, and jointly developing a professional knowledge base, teachers are better able to defend the value of their work and meet the growing demands for accountability. Each of these needs calls for con-certed action on the three levels of the individual teacher, the school and national policy. The three levels are interlinked, which is to say that the activities of the indi-vidual teacher occur in a context heavily influenced by local and national conditions.

Working guidelines for the professional development of teachers

The principles outlined above have certain practical implications for teachers and their professional development, as discussed in the seven working guidelines which follow.

1) *The more complex a professional activity becomes, the more policy interventions have to take into account the views of the practitioners and leave space for local adaptation*

The understanding here is that the practical problems of complex modern societies can rarely be solved for the local institutions by central regulation. Instead, the problem-solving capacity of these institutions and of the persons working in them has to be improved. This guideline is not always followed, however, as indicated by two different responses to a development in *Austria*, where the media had reported parental concerns about students needing more instructional help. In one province the regional administration issued a mandate that a third of the time in each lesson should be reserved for review purposes. However, in another, the regional authority sent a letter to all schools outlining the problem, inviting clarifying discussion and proposals for action, following which comments would be circulated and policy measures adopted as necessary.

2) *The closer in time, space and resource an intervention is with respect to actual teaching and learning activities, the more influence it has*

This is to imply that effective utilisation of external ideas in complex practical situations is primarily a matter of direct access to the right ideas and resources at the right moment. On this basis the local know-how available elsewhere within a teaching staff has a high potential for professional development, since it is close in a spatial sense, is likely to be accessible at the right time and is already well perceived within the local context.

3) *Innovations move along the social network of personal acquaintance*

Indirect contact suffices to spread simple, well-structured and routine information, whereas direct contact is much more effective where there is an element of uncertainty or when results are unpredictable (House, 1974). This assumption implies that informal contacts have strong effects on the dissemination of innovations and of local professional knowledge. In a complex social system the task of administration is less to provide answers to problems, than to provide contexts for personal communication through which ideas can spread. The development of strategies that encourage effective negotiation processes between sub-systems in the society may be one of the important new tasks of central administration. Thus in education it is important to stimulate communication among teachers, so that they exchange experiences and advance each other's thinking. Prerequisites would seem to include long breaks, spatial opportunities to meet inside school, and structured meetings – whether in teams or more loosely-coupled – for teachers who share common interests or responsibilities.

4)   *Innovations in complex situations cannot be cloned*

An understandable dream of the policy-maker is the replication of innovative developments which have already shown their potential, though the dream is unreal, partly because the contexts are never identical. Beyond this, however, the match between the innovation and the personal values of the teacher is at least as likely as the intrinsic quality of the innovation to determine its impact on practice. This principle implies that any substantial innovation must allow teachers to identify with it in a personal sense, to modify it in particular ways, so that it becomes their own, not merely a copy of somebody else's developments. As a consequence, professional development initiatives need to leave space for this ownership to be developed. Very often the direct access to innovative practices offers the experience that obstacles can be overcome, and promotes the exchange of ideas. This, without pressure to copy, may be more effective than offering tested materials or behavioural specifications. Thus it was concluded in *Sweden* that general solutions cannot be proposed to solve local problems, nor can general models be adapted to local conditions. It was the process by which a school set about its curriculum development that would be of interest to other schools, rather than the particular curriculum refinements adopted locally.

5)   *The challenges of complex situations demand the production of local professional knowledge in situ*

In situations which are characterised by ambiguous and partially contradictory aims, only a part of the knowledge needed can be acquired through courses, regulations and materials. A significant part must be produced by the practitioners themselves. It follows that an important professional competence is the ability to reflect on action, and in consequence to modify the approach adopted (Altrichter *et al.*, 1993).

6)   *Co-operation develops only if it is needed*

Co-operation between professionals cannot be mandated nor is it merely a result of good will. Whereas most teachers say that they dislike their isolation, co-operation only develops when the professional tasks as perceived by the teachers demand it. This has not traditionally been the case, but co-operation becomes an imperative if a dynamic culture of learning is being developed, as when teachers create links to the community or engage in interdisciplinary projects. The need for collaboration was made evident in *Danish* planning, when proposing a move away from the school day or week based on a strict division of lessons and subjects, to models with periods of topic or project work. Such models:

"would all have this in common, that they would be so wide in scope that no single person could span them all at a sufficiently high academic level, no matter how good a teacher-education they have received. This requires close co-operation within the group of teachers attached to a class, a co-operation which promotes co-ordination and the communal assumption of respon-sibility" (Denmark, 1992b, p. 250).

7) *Innovations of complex professional practices demand a systemic approach*

As long as they remain individual initiatives, constructive proposals to meet new educational challenges can neither be sustained nor can they change the edu-cational culture of schools. "Individual transformation does not spiral to whole school change unless other related pieces, such as curricula, assessments, collegial interactions, and professional development are reworked in tandem to sustain change at the classroom level. By the same token, to facilitate both whole school and individual change, a District's instructional policies and practices must be in alignment" (Slattery, 1995, p. 10). Where policy is based on technical rationality, the assumption is that innovations can be developed and tested outside schools and be transferred to them. Moves to reflective rationality, however, are based on the understanding that local initiatives exist already and that policies can support their growth process symbolically and instrumentally.

Professional development can be seen as central within school development. If this symbiotic relationship is taken seriously, schools have to be reconceptual-ised as "learning organisations" (Marx and van Ojen, 1993, p. 177), or "policy-active" institutions (Posch, 1987, p. 184). Policy-active schools are engaged in the develop-ment and realisation of an educational policy adapted to their own context, the whole school being concerned with the challenges it is facing, and involved in developing a common understanding of educational and organisational aims. The school supports a systematic reflection on its own strengths and weaknesses, in order to find constructive answers to challenges and to maximise the intellectual and creative potentials available among teachers, students, parents and the com-munity. Such a school readily accepts a responsibility for innovations which appear to be necessary in the light of its own policy. These innovations are not considered as external and potentially threatening interventions, but as natural. Professional development not only emerges from individual interests but is embedded in a shared policy. If external support is needed it is actively sought. This view of schools as learning organisations is based on the assumption that teachers – and with increasing age, students – are centrally involved in the interpretation of edu-cational aims and the construction of teaching and learning. The interactive devel-opment of aims and educational practices is a continuing responsibility of schools.

POLICIES TO SUPPORT THE PROFESSIONAL DEVELOPMENT OF TEACHERS

An important long-term aim of national policy should be to increase the involvement of schools in policy formulation, as in Ireland:

"(...) the strong message emerging consistently from all quarters is that the approach to professional and personal development should be decentralised, school-focused and conducive to high levels of teacher-participation in all aspects of the process. This is not to say that there is no role for programmes and courses external to the school, nor for actions initiated by national bodies" (Ireland, 1995, p. 127).

Professional development policies should follow and selectively support emerging local development. Many teachers are already fully involved in a change process, in advance of any policy initiatives, because of the pressing problems the new demands on teaching and learning have created for them (Specht, 1995). Innovations, especially when introducing a more dynamic learning culture, are the constructive answers of teachers to pressures experienced in their working situations. Generally, however, they are no more than the pioneer initiatives of highly involved teachers. Policies should carefully monitor emerging developments, and provide supporting contexts to those which show promise. The sections which follow give an overview of a variety of policy approaches to professional development, whether by direct intervention or indirectly through a systemic educational reform.

Curriculum-promoted professional development

If teachers are expected to develop a dynamic learning culture, the curriculum should provide space for local interpretations at school and classroom levels. In addition, there should be provisions for teachers to be actively involved in curriculum development. Thus *Italy* has introduced a project element to the curricula of technical schools (age 14-19) and upper secondary schools which have implemented the new curriculum, programme *Brocca*. The idea is to use a defined amount of school time for projects with a cross-curricular perspective, such as environmental education or multicultural education. Teachers have to work in teams to design and implement the projects, and to modify their organisation of time. In *Denmark*, the class teacher is requested "to co-operate with the students on the solution of special tasks in relation to the class" and is "allocated an extra weekly lesson with a view to carrying out this task" (Denmark, 1994, p. 10). Such a regulation is designed to help the teachers' interest in professional development.

France is currently concerned by the student failure rate at undergraduate level and by growing youth unemployment. Many school students presently engaged in general studies go straight on to unemployment. The need is seen to make selection procedures positive and improve career counselling, so that all students will engage in the courses of studies that best suit their ability and job-market capacity. Teachers will have an important role to play in the required procedures, that will mean altering their professional practice, but for this they are not well prepared. Another *French* example is the introduction of foreign language teaching in primary schools. Until recently, any foreign language teaching in primary schools was mostly carried out by secondary school teachers working extra time. Now, however, all children aged 7 to 10 are to experience fifteen minutes a day by means of audio-visual aids. This represents a real challenge, requiring a significant realignment of teachers' skills and practices. Although teachers do not have to be able to teach the language, they need some familiarity, and they need competence in the use of the new technologies.

Teacher involvement in constructing national curricula

About 100 Swedish schools – nominated as reference schools – were asked to document their experiences with the development of a local curriculum in connection with the latest national guidelines. Such approaches are expected to stimulate professional development activities in schools, and to increase the visibility of school initiatives and instructional innovations. In Austria, a curriculum innovation which had considerable impact on professional development is the government-supported Environment and School Initiatives Project (Austria, 1994b). Within this project emerged the design for a practice-based INSET workshop which was widely implemented. A procedure has been devised in France for proposed changes in the national curriculum to be circulated to individual teachers for comment. The school collects the observations of those who wish to be personally involved. Subsequently, comments pass to a regional inspector in the appropriate subject, who prepares a regional synthesis for the ministry. The comments are then taken into account before the final policy document is published. Teachers' input was at first hesitant, as they were not used to giving an opinion on such matters. It is hoped that this procedure, which takes more than a year to complete, will enable teachers to become more involved, and therefore able to identify more closely with proposed changes in giving effect to them.

In 1987, Denmark initiated a country-wide programme of educational development in order to prepare a major reform of the Folkeskole. The programme lasted for four years in order to initiate and evaluate radical changes in seven areas:

- developing the school as a local cultural centre;
- replacing the traditional divisions into lessons and subjects in favour of topic and project work, to integrate academic, practical and creative skills, and secure active student involvement in educational decision-making;
- giving to the class tutor the role of co-ordinator of all teachers attached to a class, to ensure systematic attention to the social aspects of teaching and learning;
- experimenting with new models of co-operation, both within the school and with parents and the local community;
- stimulating colleges of education to become educational centres, becoming themselves involved in school development;

- facilitating research and development, by giving schools and local authorities more freedom in the use of resources;
- the scheme had proposed that "the best possible opportunities are to be provided to allow this work of development to grow from the bottom upwards, solidly rooted in local conditions" (Denmark, 1992b, p. 252). Over 8 000 local development activities were approved, financed and evaluated.

In some countries new national curriculum structures are in preparation or already in operation, designed to stimulate professional development and the introduction of dynamic elements into the culture of teaching and learning. Examples come from the Swiss canton of Zurich (Switzerland, 1994), the German province of Bremen (Fleisch-Bickmann, 1994) and Austria. Typically such schemes have 20-40 per cent of the total time available reserved for teacher-student negotiations, and curricular prescriptions refer to a longer time-period, such as three years, to facilitate subject co-operation and create space for local variations. Subjects are defined more broadly, with topics such as "Man and the Environment", to facilitate the local legitimisation of learning activities and to increase the flexible use of teacher competences. Priority is given to aims, whilst detailed content specifications are more likely to be optional, giving exemplary scenarios of instructional approaches and student activities, against which teachers are stimulated to test options and develop their own approaches.

Such innovatory work acknowledges the process to be as important as the product. Professional development activities (primarily workshops) are not organised after the product is available but are an integral part of the development phase. Curriculum development is an element of systemic reform and not to be separated from the assessment system nor from the organisational structures of teaching and learning. As a result new forms of assessment are being developed – such as the use of portfolios – which are more in line with the dynamic elements of the culture of learning. A main thrust of all such policy initiatives is to give responsibility to schools and to stimulate them to develop their own answers to national demands.

Student assessment and professional development

Systems of student assessment are an important factor influencing teachers' professional development needs. Traditional assessment systems, particularly external ones, are based on the assumption that all students are supposed to learn the same things, e.g. bodies of knowledge defined by the traditional subject categories, and favour a specific type of professional development. As the emphasis shifts towards dynamic learning cultures this assumption becomes problematic. In an Irish evaluation report the prevailing system of public examinations was identified by teachers as one of two major obstacles to the development of a more dynamic culture of teaching and learning, the other being the time structure (Archer, 1994). When students are given the opportunities to develop their individual talents and abilities, perhaps using locally-available opportunities, new forms of assessment have to be developed.

Portfolio assessment

One promising approach is the use of a portfolio to give a "portrait" of the learner. Portfolios provide evidence of a variety of student accomplishments and document the individual strengths of the learner. An example of portfolio use is the US *Rochester City Goals* initiative, which intends, among other things, to "shift from a failure-oriented system, preoccupied with documenting deficiencies and categorising students, to one that is success-based, focused on identifying and amplifying student accomplishments" (Slattery, 1995, p. 11). It will decrease reliance on standardised multiple-choice tests in favour of performance-based assessments and teacher judgement. A similar approach is used in *Denmark*, the intention being that a school-leaving certificate shall contain information on the educational activities in which the student has participated as well as the most recent proficiency marks (Denmark, 1994, p. 7).

Using formative assessment – a French example

In *France*, there have been major developments in recent years to strengthen the use of formative assessment. It is normal for assessment to involve teachers and be used to initiate changes in professional practices. Even standardised tests are used in this way in schools. Mass diagnostic testing of core subjects is conducted at the beginning of each academic year, for all students aged 8, 11 and 16. About 800 000 students for each of the first two levels – the whole of the age group – and around 500 000 for the higher level are tested every year. These assessments of students' achievements are primarily intended for diagnostic use by teachers and parents at the school level. Assessment becomes a pedagogical tool radically different from school inspection. Exercises used in the tests are carefully itemised, to allow the measure of achievement in the various competences and skills which the national curriculum should have enabled the students to acquire the previous year. The tests, devised by national and regional working groups comprising teachers and members of the inspectorate, are administered by the form teachers. They are conducted at the beginning of the year, to provide information on students' previous achievements, which helps teachers decide what should be taught and how during the forthcoming year. The timing of the tests demonstrates that the assessment cannot reflect on the work of the current teachers, but is primarily a teaching aid.

How, then, does this assessment influence professional behaviour in the classroom? The mathematics results in the first survey of 8-year-old primary school students pointed to a national emphasis favouring arithmetic rather than geometry, even though both subjects are given equal weight in the national curriculum. When the school teachers saw these results, they drew the appropriate conclusions and altered their teaching to give more emphasis to geometry. The results of the following year's tests clearly showed that competence in geometry had greatly improved across the country, without any specific instructions being given to the teachers by the authorities. The great majority of primary and lower secondary teachers are using the assessment evidence as a source of information on students' needs. There are less upper secondary teachers doing so, reflecting differing traditions of teaching styles and classroom independence. To encourage formative assessment, with the aim of improving the quality of learning, a bank of assessment items has been made available to teachers, for use during the year on a voluntary basis according to need. Most teachers using the items have made favourable comments on their quality and usefulness.

Quality assurance and professional development

It was argued above that responsibility for the development of quality should be devolved to teachers and schools, with accountability based on a concept of reflective reaching. A major impact on professional development can be expected from policy initiatives in quality assurance.

The development of standards

Professional standards for beginning teachers in Australia were designed, in an attempt to make the work of teachers more explicit (Ruby and Rudnev, 1993), but the main illustration here again comes from France, where a national set of standard indicators has been formulated and made available to secondary schools. There are five categories:

- student-input indicators such as type of previous school, proportion of students repeating a year, personal characteristics – age, sex, socio-economic background, etc.;

- student-outcome indicators, such as success rate at *baccalauréat*, proportion of *baccalauréat* holders among all students leaving the school, where students go after leaving secondary education;

- resource indicators such as characteristics of teachers, number of teaching sessions per year provided by the school;

- organisational indicators such as class size, student progression at the end of the first year, non-teaching services provided, teacher mobility;

- environmental indicators such as relations with outside firms or companies.

The standard indicators fall into four categories: input indicators (student characteristics), output indicators (school examination results, admission of students to higher forms or higher institutions), indicators relating to resources and indicators on school management and environment. They are deliberately kept down to about twenty and constitute the background against which schools can measure themselves. From them should come an accurate description of how schools function, along with an estimate of the "value added" by each. Logically, analysis of the information provided by the indicators should lead schools to revise their policy, amongst other things in terms of admission procedures, selection, and opportunities for repeating years.

The second aspect of this programme is to provide tools which allow schools to devise their own specific indicators, that take account of individual and regional characteristics. A computer programme was developed for use with school hardware and made available to schools for the purpose. This programme should be particularly useful in helping schools to devise, implement and evaluate their own development plan, which is a legal requirement. Within the broader framework of the national curriculum and other general requirements, the development plan is meant to be the centrepiece of each school's activity. The intention is to promote serious rethinking of current practices in all areas of school, and to identify new ways of running schools. All this illustrates the coherence of the policy, designed to encourage a positive evolution of professional practices, using assessment as a pedagogical tool.

Staff development and appraisal

In *Scotland*, Local Authority schemes for staff development and appraisal follow government guidelines. After a phased introduction, the intention is for all teachers to be included in a 2-year cycle for career review and appraisal. Teachers' demands for staff development have increased as a result of career review and appraisal. More staff development is now being provided within schools or by groups of schools working together, and less through attendance at courses run by LEAs or teacher education institutions. For *England and Wales*, the Education Reform Act of 1988 triggered a number of policies designed to emphasise the importance of professional development and INSET, including arrangements for the appraisal of all serving teachers, and a requirement for staff development plans to be an essential element of whole-school plans. Regular school inspections to identify development needs are to be followed by action plans, and schools will receive grants for meeting the development needs identified. Subsequently, the Education Act of 1994 established the Teacher Training Agency to be responsible for aspects of in-service training, notably for headteachers and for new teachers (with the implementation for them of a profile of competence).

The Office for Standards in Education (OFSTED) initiated a longitudinal inspection, to determine how schools respond to INSET priorities, with particular respect to school development and action plans, to assess the impact on the quality of teaching and learning, and to examine how schools evaluate the effectiveness of INSET. Sixty primary and secondary schools were selected and received an initial full inspection in 1992-93. The published inspection reports and subsequent action plans provided the background information for the longitudinal inspection, which lasted for six months and comprised three phases: agreement on a focus and classroom visits to assess the current practice in the identified area; school visits to related INSET events; school visits to gather evidence on the impact of the training on classroom practice. It was evident that most schools had identified an INSET co-ordinator, but few of these had been trained for the role, and although INSET plans were usually linked to school development plans, few schools had written INSET policies. Schools were increasingly selective in their use of INSET providers from the public sector, but many had too little information to choose providers from the private sector.

The subsequent report dealt with how successful each school had been in meeting the target it had set itself and provides some information on the strengths and weaknesses of this approach. Most of the 50 or so INSET sessions inspected were considered satisfactory or better. The best had clearly-defined objectives that had been accepted by the participants and related closely to classroom realities; sessions included authoritative presentations, and adhered closely but not inflexibly to an agreed agenda, drawing productively on the teachers' knowledge and experience and encouraging full participation. Effective INSET stemmed from the shared commitment to raising standards of a mutually-supportive and self-critical staff; it involved detailed planning, follow-up and evaluation. Typically, however, procedures for the evaluation of INSET were unsystematic, with little attention to the impact on classroom practice: more than half the schools had unsatisfactory arrangements for disseminating what had been learned. In the majority of schools the inspectors noted some impact on teaching – such as questioning techniques, collaborative planning, awareness of different teaching methods – but only rarely improvements in students' learning and standards of work.

The US *Rochester City Goals* initiative (mentioned under "Student assessment and professional development" above) undertook an audit. A 10 per cent sample of student portfolios for review was selected at random, with a teacher from each school invited to participate. Of special interest in our context was "the reaction of participating teachers and administrators, who unequivocally stated that it was the most powerful professional development they had ever experienced" (Slattery, 1995, p. 28). The suggested national contract for teachers in Italy links the possibility of career advancement to particular professional accomplishments, such as gaining university diplomas, participating in INSET programmes or innovation projects.

Criticism arose because the quality criteria were undefined and it had not been determined whether some kind of teachers' appraisal would be linked. In the *Czech Republic* a two-level in-service certification system is planned. The system, though not obligatory, will be linked to substantial salary increases and provide access to certain educational and managerial positions, such as induction teacher, career counsellor and deputy head.

The *Irish* report entitled *Charting our Education Future* (Ireland, 1995, p. 133) anticipated a nationally-agreed framework within which schools would develop teacher-appraisal systems. Mainly the system would identify good teachers, providing opportunities for their personal and professional development and showing how their strengths could contribute to improved school performance. It was recognised, however, that the initial identification of teachers experiencing professional difficulties would arise in the same context, which led to three proposals to cope with the problem: first in-career support services would be increased, and second a teacher welfare and counselling service would be implemented. Ultimately, however, procedures would be established for termination of contract, in recognition of the harm that the few unsatisfactory teachers can cause to students and the teaching profession as a whole. A Teaching Council has been proposed, to give the teaching profession a degree of control over and responsibility for its own activities and facilitate its closer engagement in the process of change. It would exercise responsibility for the registration of serving and future teachers, and for disciplinary procedures including deregistration, in the search for the highest professional standards.

The development of quality assurance mechanisms such as these is likely to become more and more important. A basic issue will be the relationship between state-controlled, profession-controlled and consumer-controlled accountability. An institutionalised teacher contribution to the process appears indispensable if accountability is expected to contribute to the stimulation of professional development.

Infrastructures and professional development

With increasing complexity of educational tasks, the demands on the infra-structural support increase. There is a growing market offering a variety of services, of varying quality, so the chance of not getting value for money seems also to be increasing. As a result, suggestions have arisen for some sort of accreditation policy or national directory of trainers and providers of professional development. In the *Czech Republic* two nation-wide movements emerged to influence the transformation of the educational system. The "Friends of Committed Teaching" (PAU) concentrate on internal reform and new teaching methods introducing principles of liberalisation, humanisation and democratisation into school life. The "Independent

Inter-branch Group for the Reform of Educational Policy" (NEMES) is involved in a comprehensive project on system reform.

Austria has Regional Teacher Forums in which teachers are invited to present their initiatives for professional discussion, while a similar policy initiative is represented by the Australian National Teacher Forums. Teacher Centres in Ireland are expected to continue to provide a major focus for local training in the future. Their purpose is to provide a meeting place for teachers to discuss work-related issues, act as resource centres for teachers and promote in-career development. In the Netherlands there are regional guidance centres which collaborate closely with a national centre (the SLO), to give two levels of public-education support. About 40 per cent of SLO's assignments come directly from schools. Scotland offers multi-media packages such as interactive video and CD-ROM in different curriculum areas, to give flexibility in school to individuals or groups of teachers engaged in staff development. It is intended also to produce materials to support school co-ordinators in their planning of staff development programmes, to help ensure that needs are met at all levels – national, local education authority, school and individual.

The US Rochester City Goals initiative (see above) considered it vital to establish an institutional infrastructure and communication links for professional development to become integral to the routine of teaching and learning. One approach was to enhance the capacity of existing teacher networks, another to recruit additional teachers who were interested in providing leadership for a given subject area in their school. A third approach was to form committees with membership drawn from central office, building administrators and volunteer teachers, to set standards and resolve the problems of changing practice. The infrastructure provided continuity and teachers involved in on-going professional development helped to shape additional developmental opportunities for themselves and others.

Most of these initiatives require the development of communication networks among teachers. Approaches to facilitate the exchange of experience and mutual stimulation are likely to be among the most important strategies of professional development in the future. It remains to be seen how far such personal and face-to-face communication can be complemented by electronic networks.

Teacher training institutions as professional development centres

The movement towards more dynamic structures of teaching and learning has considerable implications for teacher training. In order to prepare student teachers for their new roles and to meet their demands for lifelong professional development, teacher-training institutions will have to incorporate contributions to school development. Thus, in Denmark, "Colleges of Education are to be developed into educational centres, offering to a greater degree inspiration to schools in the local area and supporting the general academic and educational development of these schools" (Denmark, 1992*b*, p. 189). In a two-year national INSET programme A*ustrian* teachers of selected subjects – English, German and science – develop and evaluate innovations in their classrooms, through action research led by interdisciplinary teams of academics and teachers. The basic principle is to identify and build on the strengths of the participating teachers, who are assisted in reflecting on and documenting their practical development work, and in contributing to a professional knowledge base through case studies.

An example of the role of a teacher-training institution to support professional development is provided by the external evaluation of an initiative undertaken by St. Patrick's College in Maynooth, I*reland*. The college supported teachers of fifteen schools to implement the Junior Certificate Curriculum introduced to Irish schools in 1989. This curriculum, with its emphasis on student initiatives and opportunities for students to engage actively with the material being learned, formed the context for developing new strategic models of in-service teacher development and for trying them out on a pilot basis. It is an example of the close relationship between curriculum development and staff development. Curriculum development is in a certain sense staff development, if schools go beyond the transmission of information. The initiative, called "Schools for Active Learning" was based on the following principles (Archer, 1994, p. 3):

- "professional development is promoted by giving teachers, principals and vice-principals opportunities to reflect critically on their own practices; by encouraging the sharing of ideas and experience with colleagues in their own and other schools, and by, in a variety of ways, involving participants in decision-making about the things that effect their work;

- the basic unit of change is the whole school and, therefore, in-service which is designed to support change is most likely effective when it targets the team of people that make up the staff of the school;

- staff-development programmes are most meaningful and effective when they are undertaken to support efforts to respond to some challenge which is currently being faced;

- much of the support which schools involved in change need can be found locally, through co-operation with other schools and with other educational agencies (education departments of universities and teachers' centres)."

These four principles translated into operational features of workshops for teachers and principals which differed considerably from familiar types of teacher development. Participants were offered opportunities to present aspects of their own practice and to engage with other participants in reflection and discussion on them. A requirement of participation was that principals, vice-principals and a significant number of teachers would commit themselves to the initiative before their schools were included. Each workshop was a direct response to a curricular change, and facilitators – recruited from participating schools – received special preparation for their task. Contacts with other schools (local clusters) were stimulated. Some of the major findings of the external evaluation including policy implications (Archer, 1994, pp. 104ff.) are discussed immediately below.

Teachers reported their confidence increased through sharing ideas and experiences and discussing common problems. Space to engage in critical reflection on one's own practice in a relaxed manner and with good rapport among the participants was regarded as essential. They reported enthusiastic adoption of the collaborative aspects of the initiative, and an openness to confrontation with new ideas. Seemingly, this stemmed from the non-threatening design of the workshops, which did not require visits to each other's classrooms. A significant finding was the development of working relationships between schools, even where those schools had previously regarded each other with suspicion. Essential preconditions for success turned out to be the careful preparation of facilitators for their work, and two aspects of the role of the director: as responsible for administrative tasks (such as scheduling workshops, convening cluster meetings, resolving practical problems) and as catalyst, encouraging and motivating facilitators.

Most teachers took ideas from the workshops and tried them out in their classrooms, but the shift from more traditional teaching methods towards the methods promoted by the initiative (*e.g.* project work, small group work) was modest, and a slight majority reported that they were not satisfied with their current use of active methods. Teachers argued, however, that their behaviour was also influenced in a variety of subtle ways which enabled new ideas and emphases to be incorporated into existing approaches. Major obstacles to change appeared to be the structure of timetables, and especially the demands of the public examinations. Moreover, there were signs that the time commitment of the facilitators could not have been sustained for much longer. For the most part, they were carrying out their tasks in their own time and without significant compensation, but there is a limit to what can be achieved by pioneering teachers in this way. Other approaches need to be found for teachers to be periodically released from class contact, to engage in in-service development work.

It was found that national curriculum reform requires much more than statements of intent for curriculum content, that to attempt too much too soon may be counter-productive, and that movements to enhance active learning are seriously undermined unless curricular changes are matched by changes in modes of assessment. Educational change is a complex, demanding, time-consuming and personally upsetting affair, which requires the unlearning of conventional attitudes, practices and assumptions, and the learning of new ones. In the light of that complexity, schools which had participated in "Schools for Active Learning" and other developmental initiatives should be utilised as on-going resources for other schools. Furthermore, the four principles used here for professional development appeared to offer feasible policy guidelines for curriculum development as well as professional development.

The importance of infrastructural support systems is likely to increase, but such systems will have to change from the predominant provider-driven to a demand-driven philosophy. They will have to create contexts in which demand can be articulated and constructively answered. Teacher-training institutions will have to relate their pre-service tasks to reconceptualised in-service responsibilities. The whole teaching profession is challenged to make the quest for quality and professional development a basic concern of its institutions. In many countries, teacher associations have been stimulated by this challenge. They have extended their interests beyond negotiations for salary and conditions of work, to proactively supporting quality development in the profession.

Schools as professional development centres

Professional development should become one of the central concerns of any school. Moreover, the anchoring of responsibility for professional development within schools appears to be not only a precondition for high quality but also highly cost-effective, releasing much energy which otherwise would require the investment of extra resources. It is, however, necessary to provide time, space, resources and organisational structures, to enable teachers to plan, develop and reflect on their work. Also important is to give experienced senior teachers new professional perspectives, offering quality-oriented career opportunities within the teaching profession.

If there is a rigid time structure, based for instance on lessons of 45 minutes, learning activities going beyond the transmission of knowledge are difficult to introduce and the interest of most teachers in professional development will be low. Similarly, if the expected time commitment of teachers is wholly taken up by their classroom work, local and co-operative professional development will also be low. Policies defining non-teaching working time to be spent in school – as introduced in Norway – are evidently important to facilitate staff collaboration.

The school development plan as a stimulus for professional development

Primary schools in the Netherlands are responsible for designing their own school policy document, the "School Work Plan", which includes the teaching and development objectives, choice, scope and structure of subjects, didactic and assessment procedures, etc. In Italy, at the beginning of the school year, each school presents its "Educational School Plan" in which the educational aims of the school and the way to achieve them are defined and discussed. The plan is defined by teachers – who are also responsible for its implementation – taking into account the following:

- the social, cultural, and economic features of the local environment;
- particular characteristics of the student population;
- the students' previous achievement in their school career;
- general aims defined in the national curriculum;
- specific aims defined by the teachers.

In addition, *Italian* schools have to define the initiatives they propose using to deal with low achievement and with student failure. Since 1995-96 they have also had to elaborate a *carta dei servizi*, a document in which all school rules and procedures are indicated. This document follows negotiation among teachers, parents, administrators and – in upper secondary schools – students.

In *France*, volunteer lower-secondary schools conducted trials with a view to providing the kind of education and teaching most appropriate to student needs. Heads and teachers were relatively free within national constraints to adapt the organisation of teaching as they saw fit. In particular, schools could decide the number of weekly teaching hours – normally centrally prescribed for all schools – and chose between 20 and 30 hours, with most around 24 hours. Within the total time, schools could decide to offer more or fewer hours in French (4 to 6), maths (3 to 5), and physical education. They were also free to organise specific teaching for under-achievers and special supervised periods where students received tuition in basic skills (using reference books, problem solving, etc.). Following evaluation, the apparent success led to extension to all first-year classes in 1995-96. The same volunteer schools continued, concentrating on flexibility in hours of teaching for each subject, special supervised periods, introduction of optional Latin classes, and preparing students to make career-relevant choice of subjects.

All *French* schools are required by the 1989 Education Act to produce their own development plan, incorporating national regulations and local interests. The intention is for heads and teachers to work together on devising the plan. Traditionally, however, French teachers work alone, particularly in secondary education. They are not accustomed to working with colleagues, even in their own subject. The plan is therefore a way to promote collective initiative and concerted effort and to ensure that student requirements are taken into consideration. It has to be approved by the minister's representative in the district and is updated from time to time.

In-service education defined as professional responsibility

It is *Swedish* policy for teachers to participate in the planning of in-service training in accordance with the local school development plan. Teachers' professional development thus coincides with the development of the local curriculum. It is recognised that teachers can no longer rely on their traditional source of authority, as subject experts, but need the collegial authority which arises from the development of consensus regarding the purpose of schooling, the selection of content and the organising of activities. *Scottish* schools have five in-service days per year and teachers have the equivalent of another 50 hours to pursue their own professional development. In each school a senior staff member acts as staff development co-ordinator with the responsibility for drawing up a programme to meet staff-development needs. Teachers identify their own such needs through the career review and appraisal process. Award-bearing courses offered on a modular basis range from certificates to diplomas and master's degrees. Most teachers taking these post-qualifying courses pay the costs themselves and take the courses in their own time.

Team structures

The creation of team responsibilities causes changes in the work patterns of individual teachers that stimulate local professional development initiatives. A prominent example is the establishment of "system work units" with teams of teachers working in collaboration with groups of students (see, *e.g.*, Ruby and Rudnev, 1993, p. 4). Such structures, which facilitate team-work and mutual learning, appear to encourage teachers to regard professional development as their own responsibility. The emergence of such semi-autonomous units may be regarded as a main characteristic of learning organisations. *Denmark* now requires interdisciplinary work in teams, so the identification of good teachers to act as consultants or team leaders has become a major task for school leaders. Most countries see school principals as key personnel in stimulating professional development. Thus *Ireland* expects that, by the end of the decade, every school principal will have participated in a development programme. In *England and Wales*, the government has announced its intention to introduce a specific qualification for promotion to headteacher and a new initiative for headteacher training is being developed. These innovations reflect the understanding that headteachers play a crucial role in improving schools.

Designated resources for professional development

When teachers or schools receive money to cover the operational costs of school initiatives for professional development, as in *Denmark*, it appears to be highly cost-effective. In many cases, the main stimulating factor for the teachers may be not the amount of money made available – which is often rather small – but the symbolic acknowledgement of their work. *Austrian* schools can claim part of the financial resources of the regional pedagogical institutes (the main INSET providers) for their INSET needs, a development which has stimulated the development of school-based professional development policies. A specific policy initiative is the Austrian "Environmental Education Fund", to which teachers apply for grants to cover the operational costs of the school's environmental initiatives. The fund, which defines quality criteria and provides expert advice, became an important opportunity for the government to influence innovative developments, and stimulated the emergence of networks of teachers with similar interests.

Schools maintained by local education authorities (LEAs) in England and Wales increasingly receive financial resources directed towards new priorities, of which about half is expected to be spent on staff training. Individual Italian schools which organise professional development initiatives have access to financial resources via the provincial branches of the Ministry of Education. The Czech Republic has largely transferred INSET responsibilities to schools, which are expected to link training provisions to their "Human Resource Development Plan" (itself part of the School Plan). Funds are allocated to schools, which select the required type of training and the provider. Schools are held accountable for the use of these funds and are required to publish all relevant data in their yearly report (Czech Republic, 1995b). In France, internal competition for teaching posts appears to be a strong incentive to engage in professional development to upgrade skills.

CONCLUDING OBSERVATIONS

The discussions on teacher professionalism have ranged widely, but most of the policy initiatives described here can be regarded as steps towards policy-active schools. In these schools, continuing professional development is seen as one of the central means to cope with challenges and to improve the quality of the service. The following are some of the key features associated with such development:

- school development should be seen as prestigious, an important aspect of the task of headteachers and school staffs;

- time is needed by teachers for reflection, communication and development;

- co-operative structures must be in place, such as task groups with specific responsibilities;

- financial resources, linked to specific quality standards, must be negotiable on application;

- career opportunities and other incentives are needed to encourage highly-committed and well-qualified teachers.

Evidently, the development and continuation of policy-active schools require adequate attention to each of these five points. Once that has been achieved further systemic consideration will be possible, to ensure the best deployment of finite resources and the means by which accountability can be secured without crippling local initiatives.

THE MEMBERSHIP OF THE THREE CLUSTERS

(April 1995)

Curriculum Aims, Principles and Structures

Mr. Jos Letschert (Netherlands) – Coordinator
Mr. Joe Conaty (United States)
Ms. Rita Dunon (Belgium)
Mr. Roger-Francois Gauthier (France)
Mrs. Ines Miret (Spain)
Mrs. Maria Do Ceu Neves Roldao (Portugal)
Mr. Douglas Osler (Scotland)
Mrs. Martine Safra (France)
Mr. Otmar Schiessl (Germany)
Mrs. Ellen Marie Skaflestad (Norway)
Mrs. Elisabeth Stanzel-Tischler (Austria)
Mr. Pentti Takala (Finland)

The Curriculum and Assessment – The Need for Systemic Analysis

Dr. David Stevenson (United States) – Coordinator
Prof. Eva Baker (United States)
Mrs. Carmen Corral (Spain)
Mrs. Chiara Croce (Italy)
Mrs. Ma Luz Garcia (Spain)
Prof. Dr. Karl-Heinz Gruber (Austria)
Mrs. Dorte Heurlin (Denmark)
Mr. James Irving (New Zealand)
Mr. Melis Melissen (Netherlands)
Dr. Lenora Perry-Fagan (Canada)
Mr. John Singh (United Kingdom)

Teachers and their Professional Development

Mr. John Townshend (OECD/CERI) – Coordinator
Mr. Gerard Bonnet (France)
Prof. Ingrid Carlgren (Sweden)
Mr. Emir Egan (Ireland)
Mr. K. Fairweather (Scotland)

Mrs. Berit Hörnquist (Sweden)
Mr. Bruno Losito (Italy)
Mr. P. Muschamp (England)
Mr. Peter Posch (Austria)

In addition, the cluster groups were assisted by members of the OECD Secretariat and external experts, including Prof. J.M. Atkin (United States) and Prof. P.J. Black (United Kingdom).

BIBLIOGRAPHY

ALTRICHTER, H., POSCH, P. and SOMEKH, B. (1993), *Teachers Investigate their Work. An Introduction to the Methods of Action Research*, Routledge, London.

ARCHER, P. (1994), "An external evaluation of schools for active learning", Primatestown, Ireland.

ARGYRIS, C. and SCHÖN, D. (1974), *Organisational Learning*, Addison-Wesley, Reading, Massachussetts.

AUSTRIA (1994a), *Berufswahl von Mädchen, Perspektiven-Hindernisse-Konzepte*, Dokumentation einer Enquete, Bundesministerium für Unterricht und Kunst, Vienna.

AUSTRIA (1994b), *Seminarmodell Schlaining – Projektunterricht – Sinnerfülltes Lehren und Lernen*, BMUK, Bundesministerium für Unterricht und Kunst, Vienna (Medienbegleitheft zum Video, Reg. No. 86018).

BEGIN, M. and CAPLAN, G.L. (1994), *For the Love of Learning*, Report of the Royal Commission on Learning, Ontario.

BLACK, P.J. and ATKIN, J.M. (1996), *Changing the Subject: Innovations in Science, Mathematics and Technology Education*, OECD/Routledge, London.

BRUNER, J. (1990), *Acts of Meaning*, Harvard University Press, Cambridge, Massachussetts and London.

CORNELIS, F. (1994), *Education for Europeans: Towards the Learning Society*, European Round Table of Industrialists, Brussels.

CZECH REPUBLIC (1995a), *Quality and Accountability: The Programme of Development of the Education System in the Czech Republic*, Ministry of Education, Youth and Sports, Prague.

CZECH REPUBLIC (1995b), "The Ministry's programme: the teacher", Ministry of Education, Youth and Sports, Prague.

DENMARK (1992a), *Statement of Educational Policy*, Folkeskolen Udviklingsrad, Copenhagen.

DENMARK (1992b), *The Danish Folkeskole: Visions and Consequences*, Folkeskolen Udviklingsrad, Copenhagen.

DENMARK (1994), *Act on the Folkeskole*, Danish Ministry of Education, Copenhagen.

DOLL, W.A. Jr. (1993), *A Post-modern Perspective on Curriculum*, Teachers College Press, New York and London.

ELLIOTT, J. (1983), "Self-evaluation, professional development, and accountability", in Galton, M. and Moon, B. (eds.), *Changing Schools, Changing Curriculum*, Harper and Row, London, pp. 224-247.

ELLIOTT, J. (1994), "Developing community-focused environmental education through action research", *Evaluation and Innovation in Environmental Education*, OECD/CERI, Paris.

ENDT, E. and HOOGHOFF, H. (eds.) (1994), "Report on the Fifth International Symposium", *The European Dimension in Education*, Enschede, Dillingen, Dundee.

FINLAND (1994), *Framework Curriculum for the Comprehensive School 1994*, National Board of Education, Helsinki.

FLEISCH-BICKMANN, W. (1994), "Rahmenplan und Schulcurriculum – Einen Konsens über päda-gogische Fragen und Zieosetzungen gemeinsam tragen", *Schulleitung und Schulentwicklung*, September, pp. 1-21.

GOODLAD, J.I. (1979), *Curriculum Inquiry: The Study of Curriculum Practice*, McGraw-Hill, New York.

HANDY, C. (1989), *The Age of Unreason*, Business Books, London.

HOUSE, E. (1974), *The Politics of Educational Innovation*, McCutchan, Berkeley.

IRELAND (1995), *Charting our Education Future*, White Paper, Dublin.

JAPAN (1994), *Japanese Government Policies in Education, Science and Culture 1994: New Directions in School Education, Fostering Strength for Life*, Monbusho (Ministry of Education, Science, Sports and Culture), Tokyo.

LARCHER, D. (1995), "Lernkultur statt Zielerreichung – Aus der Praxis eines offenen Curricu-lums", Universität Klagenfurt.

LICKONA, T. (1993), "The return of character education", *Educational Leadership*, ASCD, Vol. 51, No. 3.

LORTIE, D.C. (1975), *School Teacher. A Sociological Study*, University of Chicago Press, Chicago.

MARX, E.C.H and van OJEN, Q.H.J.M. (1993), "Dezentralisation, Deregulierung und Autono-misierung im niederländischen Schulsystem", in Posch, P. and Altrichter, H. (eds.), *Schulau-tonomie in Österreich, Bundesministerium für Unterricht und Kunst*, pp. 162-185.

MORAVEC, P. (1994), "Austria: development of education", Report presented at the 44th session of the International Conference on Education, Geneva.

OECD (1990), *Reviews of National Policies for Education: Norway*, Paris.

OECD (1994), *The OECD Jobs Study: Facts, Analysis, Strategies*, Paris.

OECD (1995a), *Performance Standards in Education: In Search of Quality*, Paris.

OECD (1995b), *Literacy, Economy and Society: Results of the First International Adult Literacy Survey*, Paris.

OECD (1996), *Lifelong Learning for All*, Paris.

OECD/CERI (1990), *Curriculum Reform: An Overview of Trends*, Paris.

OECD/CERI (1991), *Environment, Schools and Active Learning*, Paris.

OECD/CERI (1993), *Curriculum Reform: Assessment in Question*, Paris.

OECD/CERI (1994), *The Curriculum Redefined: Schooling for the 21st Century*, Paris.

OECD/CERI (1995a), *Measuring the Quality of Schools*, bilingual, Paris.

OECD/CERI (1995b), *Schools under Scrutiny*, Paris.

OECD/CERI (1995c), *Integrating Students with Special Needs into Mainstream Schools*, Paris.

OECD/CERI (1995d), *Our Children at Risk*, Paris.

OECD/CERI (1997a), *Education at a Glance 1997 – OECD Indicators*, Paris

OECD/CERI (1997b), *Implementing Inclusive Education*, Paris.

PINAR, W.F., REYNOLDS, W.M., SLATTERY, P. and TAUBMAN, P.M. (1995), *Understanding Curricu-lum: An Introduction to the Study of Historical and Contemporary Curriculum Discourses*, Peter Lang Publishing Inc., New York.

PORTUGAL (1993), *Portuguese Education Act* (Law 46/86 of 14 October), Ministry of Education, Lisbon.

POSCH, P. (1987), "The assimilation perspective", in Miles M.B., Ekholm, M. and Vandenberghe, R. (eds.), *Lasting School Improvement – Exploring the Process of Institutionalisation*, Acco, Leuven, pp. 173-188.

POSCH, P. (1994), "Networking in environmental education", *Evaluation and Innovation in Environ-mental Education*, OECD/CERI, Paris, pp. 61-87.

POSCH, P. and ALTRICHTER, H. (1992), *Bildung in Österreich – Analysen und Entwicklungsperspek-tiven*, Österreichischer Studienverlag, Innsbrück.

REID, W.A. (1994), "Curriculum planning as deliberation", Report No. 11, Pedagogisk Forskningsinstitutt, University of Oslo.

ROCHA TRINDADE, M.B. and SOBRAL MEDES, M.L. (1993), "Portugal, a profile of intercultural education", *European Journal of Intercultural Studies*, Vol. 4, No. 2.

RUBY, A. and RUDNEV, L. (1993), "Restructuring the profession: why Australia should value its teachers", Paper prepared for the Australian College of Education National Conference.

SCHÖN, D. (1983), *The Reflective Practitioner*, Temple Smith, London.

SCOTLAND (1992), *Thinking European: Ideas for Integrating a European Dimension into the Curriculum*, Scottish Consultative Council on the Curriculum, Dundee.

SLATTERY, J.B. (1995), "The Rochester City School District's goals initiative: a case study in the making", Rochester.

SLO (National Institute for Curriculum Development) (1994), *Basic Education in the Netherlands*, Ministry of Education, Zoetermeer.

SPAIN (1994), *Education: National Report*, Ministry of Education and Science, Presented at the International Conference on Education in Geneva.

SPECHT, W. (1995), "Qualität der Schule: Qualität der Schulsystems", in Specht W. and Thonhauser, J. (eds.), *Schulqualität*, Bundesverlag, Vienna.

STANDAERT, R. (1990), *De vlag in de top. Over de "rationaliteit" van het secundair onderwijsbeleid, Frankrijk, Engeland en Wales, Duitse Bondsrepubliek* (The flag in top. About the "rationality" of secondary education in France, England and Wales, and Germany), Acco, Leuven.

STENHOUSE, L. (1975), *An Introduction to Curriculum Research and Development*, Heinemann, London.

SWEDEN (1995), *Directives of the Commission on the Inner Work of the School*, Ministry of Education and Science, Stockholm.

SWITZERLAND (1994), *Volksschullehrplan des Kantons Zurich*, Erziehungsdepartement, Zürich.

TENBRUCK, F. (1975), "Der Fortschritt der Wissenschaft als Trivialisierungsprozess", in Steer, N. and König, R. (eds.), *Wissenschaftssoziologie*, Kölner Zeitschrift für Soziologie und Sozialpsychologie, Vol. 18, pp. 19-47.

WALKER, D.C. (1990), *Fundamentals of Curriculum*, Harcourt Brace Jovanovich Inc., United States.

WARNOCK, M. (1978), *Report of the Committee of Enquiry into the Education of Handicapped Children and Young People* (The Warnock Report), HMSO, London.

WEYNS, W. (1990), *De sociologie van Jürgen Habermas* (The sociology of Jürgen Habermas), Acco, Leuven/Amersfoort.

WIELEMANS, W. (1995), "Eindtermen: tussen culturele identiteit en wereldburgerschap" (Core objectives: between cultural identity and world citizenship), *Impuls*, Vol. 25, No. 4, Acco, Leuven.

OECD PUBLICATIONS, 2, rue André-Pascal, 75775 PARIS CEDEX 16
PRINTED IN FRANCE
(96 98 06 1 P) ISBN 92-64-16141-4 – No. 50295   1998